West of Hue

Down the Yellow Brick Road

Recollections of a Recondo in Vietnam

Written by:
James P. Brinker

West of Hue
Down the Yellow Brick Road

by

James P. Brinker

Published by

Brundage Publishing
Room 203 Executive Office Building
33 West State Street
Binghamton, NY 13901

www.brundagepublishing.com

Jacket design by: Barrie Hoople

Library of Congress
Control Number: 2004102808

ISBN Number: 1-892451-19-0

Printed in the United States of America

Dedication

This book of personal memories is dedicated to the memory of the following fallen men from the Reconnaissance Platoon 2/502 101st Airborne Division KIA 1970. Their memory will live on in the hearts of all who knew them, for they were the best America could give.

Marlin Trent Peterson
Harold William Shuler
Raymond Ross Moon
Steven Roy Sandlin
John Allen Claggett
Robert Emmet Cain
Gary Wayne Gear
Russell LeRoy Bahrke Jr.

The following from 1970 have joined their Recon Brothers on the yellow brick road in Heaven:

James Turnbull, 1972
Fenton B. Flying "Chief", 1988
Doc Michael L. Ackerman, 1990
John A. Underhill, 1999
Diamon Kelly Torres, 2000
Bernard V. Slider, Jr., 2003
Clarence F. Cogdell, 2004

i

Acknowledgements

Thank you to the Brundage Publishing staff members David Ortiz, Jennifer Sembler, and Barrie Hoople for their outstanding work in putting my book together. It was obvious from the start that you soon became more than workers, and that you had your hearts in this endeavor.

Author in Nam, 1970

Author going out on bunker line duty
"Night of the Rockets"

Ron "Sid" Mease, author, unknown

Author at Bach Ma

HEADQUARTERS
RECONDO FORCE
Republic of Vietnam

TO ALL WHO SEE THESE PRESENTS, GREETINGS:

This is to certify that

The Commanding Officer of the Recondo Force
2d Battalion (Airborne) 502d Infantry
1st Brigade, 101st Airborne Division
has this day admitted

JAMES PHILLIP BRINKER

to

_____lifetime_____membership into the organization
Known as

THE RECONDO FORCE
and is entitled to all the privileges
and benefits of this elite group.

Given under my hand in the Republic of Vietnam,
Airborne Country, Widowmaker Territory,
Recondo Area of Operations

This____8th____day of_November_____19_70_

Commanding
JAMES A. CATLIN
CPT, Infantry
Commanding

"SPEARHEADING THE STRIKE FORCE"

Table of Contents

How soon hath time, the subtle thief of youth, stolen on his winging my three-and-twentieth year!

--John Milton

Preface

It took over thirty years to write down the events of my tour of duty in the late Republic of Viet Nam. When I returned home in November of 1970 most of my thoughts and memories along with my photographs, papers, and awards were placed in a box and pushed to the back of the closet. Most of what I knew was still classified information and I had taken an oath of secrecy in November of 1970. Once in a while something would bring back a memory or two, but the memories would always be purposely put aside. There were busy times in my life when memories of Viet Nam weren't addressed for as long as a year. All this would change in the year 2000.

Many things happened in a very short period of time and all would focus together in a surge of repressed memories. In the early part of the year 2000, one of my sons had a friend named Emily; I also had a friend named Emily in my last few months at Iowa State University.

A friend of mine died unexpectedly and this also brought back reminders of deaths long ago. I was given an article about a friend and classmate that disappeared into the jungles of Viet Nam a short time before I went there and the 25th anniversary of the end of the war had a lot of media attention and seemed to bombard me on a daily basis.

My position at work was temporarily eliminated and I came under a lot of stress. On Memorial Day, I was honored as a military veteran to lay a wreath in a local ceremony. Rifle salutes were fired and I almost broke down. I made a quick exit to save embarrassment.

After that, the flood of thoughts was almost constant. I had what some would call Post-Traumatic Stress Disorder (PTSD). This is a very common occurrence among veterans especially those who served in Viet Nam. I was still coping and thought I was still in control, but I wasn't. Hours were spent digging through my old photos, papers, and souvenirs from Viet Nam. I started to look on the Internet for friends who had been forgotten or ignored for years. Fellow Iowan Chuck Kinsey of Boone, IA from my Recon unit had his name posted on the 101st Airborne Division Association web page. I made contact with him. I posted my own name and hoped to find a guy or two. The worst was yet to come.

Within a few weeks of posting my name, and just an hour before leaving on a vacation, a man from Las Vegas sent me an inquiry about the loss of his friend in Vietnam on May 20, 1970. The message slammed into me with unbelievable force. That particular day had been the darkest day of my life. I told him that I would respond after I had some time to collect my thoughts.

Now the worst of the thoughts came rolling in. That week I visited with Chuck Kinsey. He had relocated from Boone, Iowa to Springfield, Missouri a few years before. It was the first time we had met in thirty years. A week later, I sent a short recollection to the guy in Las Vegas about the loss of his friend. It was tough to write, but it was the start of a healing process. Other stories and thoughts were soon being sent out and stories were being exchanged with many other vets. I was starting to feel a little better after getting memories and experiences out in the open. Eventually I composed a series of my memories to send out to other vets. That was the beginning of this personal story.

The language used in this account will be that of a "grunt" from "the Nam." It will be vulgar at times. After thirty-one years "It don't mean nuttin." The word "GOOK" or "DINK" will be used liberally to describe soldiers of communist North Viet Nam because they were the most often used by the common soldier. These words are not intended to slur any ethnic group,

Vietnamese or other. The politically correct term would now be North Vietnamese Army or People's Army of Viet Nam. There will be graphic descriptions of close combat. The names of the men involved in such action will be shielded so as not to embarrass them. It would be unfair to brave combat veterans to have their family and friends see where they "stitched a gook with a Mike16."

It was not my intent to write a Battalion history of these battles, although the story should be told about the thirty guys who died in one month on Hills 714 and 882. These battles were not reported extensively because of the invasion of Cambodia in 1970 and later the Kent State fiasco.

Virtually all of it is from my own memory. Certain of the worst details shamed me; I had forgotten how hardcore I had been. Some information was gleaned from official records. My Strike Force comrades or others gave some details to me. They will also be shielded to protect them. Their names will be listed as a source of information. I can authenticate virtually all of the incidents if there are any doubters. The official records are far from perfect and there is one incident not mentioned.

There were at least four other James Brinkers who served in the late Republic of Viet Nam. Hopefully none of them will suffer any embarrassment by this undertaking. One must remember that every Vietnam Veteran has a different story. This is my story.

PART ONE:

BEFORE THE WAR

Chapter 1

MILITARY HERITAGE

Vietnam wasn't the first war to touch my family. My mother lost two brothers in WWII. Vernon Bock was KIA on Attu Island and Donald Bock was MIA as a tail gunner in a B-24 that was shot down over Albania. I saw my two uncles' photographs every time I visited my grandparents. These photographs reminded me, from a very early age, that many soldiers don't come home from wars. Although they died before I was born, I could see how their loss had continually affected my family. Until WWII, my family had very little military history. On my Father's side, one family member apparently was a non-combat death in the civil war and may have been Confederate. Family lore says some of my ancestors came to America to evade military service in Imperial Germany. Several uncles by marriage were Veterans of WWII and the Korean War.

Glidden, Iowa is where I lived all of my later childhood. It's a small prairie town in Carroll County Iowa and has a rich military history. Paul W. Tibbets Jr. named the B-29 that decisively ended WWII after his mother who once lived in Glidden. Another piece of local history is a *National Monument Honoring Meryl Hay*, one of the first three US soldiers killed in

2

WWI. Meryl Hay is little known outside the state of Iowa. In Des Moines, there is a boulevard and adjacent mall named for him. Another young man from the Glidden area named Donald Lee Sparks was missing in action during the Vietnam War and later listed as a prisoner of war. The circumstances of his disappearance in Vietnam are still being debated. Don was a fine guy and a close friend of mine.

Despite this compelling military history, the idea of military service bothered me a lot even at that early age. Joining ROTC at Iowa State once crossed my mind at the beginning of my freshman year. However the thought of going to class one day a week in a military uniform didn't appeal to me. I had little interest in anything military.

The first time I remembered anything about Viet Nam was in Annunciation grade school during a geography class in Coon Rapids, Iowa. We were taught that the country was temporarily divided and that many people, especially Catholics, had fled to the southern part of the country, which eventually became the Republic of Viet Nam. Never in my wildest dreams did I ever imagine personally seeing this spot on the globe or meeting some of these very same refugees around Hue.

Years later in 1962, TV news broadcasts started reporting about a local war in Laos and South Viet Nam; Viet Nam was still millions of miles away from me. By then I was a teenager and I knew of a student who graduated a few years before from Glidden-Ralston Community High School who had gone to Viet Nam. Now at last there was some local connection to this distant land.

I didn't have to worry about it as I had two more years of high school and college after that. Most hometown guys went to Korea or Germany if they were going overseas in the early sixties. In my sophomore year at Iowa State, my politically conservative senior roommate started talking about Nam quite a bit. Comments about the Marines kicking butt in the Iron Triangle were common.

He soon enrolled in graduate school and postponed or rather *evaded* going into the military service. A familiar pattern was already developing. Campus radicals were very active, but I

3

was very turned off by their anti-Americanism and slovenly habits. When I was in Adelante Fraternity at Iowa State we had quite a few ROTC men. Very few were planning on infantry. I still had two more years of college and if necessary graduate school was always an option. It seemed as if everyone was working on an angle to escape the military or get into some safe part of the military service. Some plans worked and others didn't.

In my junior year at Adelante Fraternity we had a Vietnamese guy living in the house. He was the first person from that country I met. His dad was a wealthy man that had recently immigrated to this country. I never asked him why the family had moved here. It was obvious that they had little faith in the Republic of Viet Nam government. The Tet holiday offensive of early 1968 woke me up a bit as I was scheduled to graduate in the fall of '68 and Graduate school was no longer an exemption from the draft, but I still had some time left. In the late spring of 1968, I realized that military service was probably going to be in my near future.

In the early autumn of 1968, I met one of the nicest girls in the world during my last days as a civilian. She was a Pi Phi with a lot of class and humor. We were quite a platonic couple. She probably thought I was heading to the Priesthood. I came back to Ames once to see her after I started student teaching. She was very nice but only a fool would start a romance just before leaving for boot camp.

On graduation day I wanted very much to go over and tell her what was going on in my mind. I went home and a few days later visited the Army recruiter. Since I had a degree in biology, going into a medical laboratory program seemed a sensible thing. I enlisted in the program and passed the exam easily. I would enter the US Army on February 7th, 1969.

4

Chapter 2

EVASION

After Basic Training was finished, medical laboratory school would start. Three years of my life in exchange for a certification and some experience was the rationale. No camping in the jungle for this kid. Those three years seemed like a million to a guy with no interest in the military.

The first problem was the military physical. The recruiter sent me to Des Moines and I passed it without any problems. The day that I got back I found a letter waiting for me. It was a draft notice and I had to report for a physical at Omaha in one week. I called the draft board and explained that I just got back from a physical in Des Moines and had already enlisted in the US Army. Barbera Hanks told me if my papers got back from Des Moines I wouldn't have to take a second physical. The papers for my physical at Ft. Des Moines were late in getting back to the draft board in Carroll County.

Worse yet, because I now had experience in taking physicals and also was one of the older guys, they put me in charge of the whole busload of Carroll County farm boys going to Omaha. It was a long trip in a bus full of mostly sullen guys. One guy talked the whole way that they were never going to get him. He appeared to be either a pure coward or knew the future, but was definitely not a conscientious objector. The guys eventually lightened up a bit, and we had some fun whenever there was an opportunity. This was mostly at the expense of a couple of effeminate medics. The best joke pulled was over-filling the urine cup. It really upset the medics when you handed it to them. Iowans were that way, always looking for some way to cause trouble.

I could have probably beaten the physical by smuggling in some animal protein and putting a little in the cup. What was wrong with me? I had this great idea that only a biologist would figure out and I didn't use it. One guy was a few pounds under weight for his height. They made him eat some bananas and drink some juice.

Donald Sparks, a friend from my high school class at Glidden-Ralston and also at Iowa State University, was finishing up his physical when I arrived. We spoke a few words and some guy yelled at us to cut the conversation off. He was very upbeat at the time. Neither of us realized what was in store for him.

A very athletic guy from my high school didn't pass the physical because of bone defects in his trigger hand and a few guys were held over for more tests. When I got home, a parent of a boy that I knew called me asking what happened to her son. I told her that it could only be good news. No one had given me a list of people that didn't pass the physical that day. As it turned out he didn't pass it.

My brother Clayton got me a temporary job at American Trampoline. They needed a guy for the holiday season rush. I told them I could work for two months. New Years Eve of 1968 was to be my going away party but I didn't know it. Don Sparks was home on leave and we said goodbye on the highway by Templeton, IA. New Year's Day morning was cold and bright just like our optimism. That was the last time I ever saw Don.

A few days later a letter arrived ordering me to report January 7th. This came as a surprise as I was expecting to go on February 7th, 1969. I assumed they had started another class a month earlier. I quit my job at the factory. The weather was terrible in Iowa and I was glad to be leaving. Two inches of ice

6

were on all the roads, but my early journey ahead would bury me like snow.

Chapter 3

CONFRONTED WITH DECISIONS

I took a bus down to Des Moines, but instead of going directly to Ft. Des Moines induction center I decided to visit a friend from the Carroll area that had moved there. While sitting on the bus, a sailor and I started talking. Soon he told me that he was a Navy SEAL and that he had a "big war story." The story ended with him killing a fellow American to put him out of his misery. I saw that he wasn't wearing the Trident of a SEAL. Over thirty years later pretend heroes are still telling similar outrageous stories.

Report time was 7:00 a.m. the next morning, but you could check in the night before and get a cot to sleep on. I took a cab over to Ft. Des Moines from my friend's apartment at about 9:00 p.m. Three of my fraternity brothers from Iowa State University showed up and I learned that two of them were going into the service. I later would go all the way through Basic Training with two buddies, Dale Schultz and Ray Vaske from Adelante Fraternity.

There were several hundred young Iowans there and that meant trouble was brewing. Sure enough, at lights out time a pillow fight started. Some "crusty old Sarge" came in and gave us the old line that anyone acting up would get infantry and

8

orders to go to Nam for sure. That calmed things up for a while until someone laughed heartily in the dark and asked, "Do you believe that guy? We're all going to Nam!"

The next day after a full day of paper shuffling they called me out of the group to talk to me. A very professional Sergeant told me that a mistake had been made, and I had been called up exactly one month too early. When I asked him what my options were he said that I had three: come back in a month or find a different field (MOS) in the Army. I asked what the third one was, and he said it was a two-year regular Army enlistment. When I asked how that differed from the draft he said that I would never be a Marine and I could leave today. I later found that it had one other advantage. The letters RA in front of your service number in those days separated you from the drafties whose service numbers had US for a starter. A few months later everyone used their social security as their service number. Almost no KP was given to "Regular Army" guys.

After about an hour of soul searching and research in the big Army MOS book, I came to a decision to take the two-year enlistment. Specialty classes wouldn't start in the time frame, or they were in fields that I had no interest in. Going back home and just sitting around in an Iowa winter didn't sound good either.

There is another explanation that I now need to face. Maybe I really wanted to go to Nam and see what all the fuss was about. It was a mistake that a year later I would look back on with regret and wish that I had gone home and looked at snow and ice for a month. The papers were signed and an oath was taken. The US Army owned me for two years.

Chapter 4

TEXAS CHEERLEADER

We were all driven over to the Des Moines airport and flown to Dallas. We had some time to kill at Dallas-Fort Worth International, so several of us slipped into an airport bar while taking turns at lookout. We had learned some military techniques already. They had put some other guy in charge this time. The next flight was on a TTA turboprop. TTA stood for Trans Texas Airlines. Most soldiers called it Tree Top Airlines in those days.

I found myself being served by a stewardess with a strange story. Within moments after being airborne she told everybody that they had fired her, but they hadn't found a replacement yet so they kept her on. They fired her for being too friendly with the soldiers. Before the flight was over she was kissing some guy in the back row. Exactly what was too friendly? She had a great idea that never caught on in other airlines.

The flight into Ft. Polk or Ft. Puke as we later called it was at night, and we could see the trees below us. Iowans are not used to a forest of conifers so it was kind of nice at first. I later grew to hate pine trees and that part of Louisiana. It was very warm when we arrived, and some of us got tired of standing around in the middle of the night and rested on an asphalt road. It was much better than Iowa in January. A day later when the unusual warm spell left, it became colder than normal and they had to issue extra blankets.

Chapter 5

NEW BEGINNINGS

For some reason the Iowa State flag was flying upside down. Maybe it was in mourning for all the Iowans arriving at Ft. Polk. Later I found out that it was indeed a distress sign. Part of the military process was to discover anything about our past criminal records if any. We Iowans had an excellent record until one guy from our group asked if we had to mention being caught with possession of liquor as a minor. An arrogant corporal with an "Arkie" twang asked everyone to raise their hands if they had been caught drinking. Virtually all the Iowans raised their hands. The corporal said, "Don't yuose nawthenaars have any hallaar treees to hides yuose licker."

That guy also got his jollies by having all the US (draftees) guys raise their hands, then the RAs, and finally the NGs. He then stated that NG stands for "No Guts" and not National Guard. Somehow the Army Reserve (AR) guys got missed.

Some of the NG guys had a real bad trick played on them. They were pulled out for a week of extra KP. This meant that the number of weeks they scheduled to be absent from their jobs had to be lengthened by a week. One guy that I was with in Basic

12

Training was the son of a factory owner in Iowa. He spent an extra week down there.

The Sergeants always had some way of entertaining themselves. A guy named Ator didn't answer when they called him the first time. They then made him shout out his name after each guy they called. He had to yell his name hundreds of times. A year later I saw his name on the casualty lists from Vietnam and assumed he was dead. I found out thirty years later that it was another guy with the same name.

The great tragedy in the induction center was missing Joe Namath and the Jets beat the Colts in the Super Bowl and I was so naïve and young not to see the true reality of my situation.

After about a week in the induction center, 200 guys dressed in green and with new haircuts were marched over to a training company. The drill instructors, or DIs as more commonly called, divided us into platoons. They made a huge oversight placing all the Iowans in one single platoon and we were assigned a very short and not too bright DI who managed to have more problems than all of us put together.

Many men knew each other within this Platoon and things went along smoothly for a while. We played the game and didn't get indoctrinated as much as the others. Ray Vaske and two other Iowans, Jim Walter and Dave Hoover, were going into helicopter flight school to become warrant officers. Jim was my bunkmate. Unknown to both of us, our paths would cross again in a little over a year.

Most guys in our company were from the central part of the US. The exception was a platoon of National Guards from NY and NJ. We frequently feuded with these eastern elitists. They actually found a way into the NG in order to avoid Vietnam. Deep down I knew I had played the same games.

One day, weeks before the end of basic, half of us were pulled out and sent to a class on M16 familiarization. This could only mean one thing. I was going into infantry. In all of basic we had used the M-14. I soon learned that my intuition was right. About one day before Basic Training was over, our orders arrived. I was sent to a two-week leadership course before going to advanced infantry training.

13

One officer told us in an informal moment that college graduates that "didn't give a damn" were being groomed for leadership roles. We were asked if we had any interest in becoming officers and going through officer candidate's school or OCS. That would mean enlisting for a third year. No hands went up. He had us pegged. This was the same way Jim Calley of Mai Lai infamy was selected for officer candidate school.

During Basic Training, I heard that a grade school friend had died in a car accident. It was always shocking news to hear about a friend's death. I heard the story several times that being in the military during the Vietnam War was just as safe as a civilian driving a car in the US. This may have been true in numbers if the worldwide number of servicemen in all branches of the service were added up, but in Nam only a low percentage of the men were in actual combat units and the combat death rate was very high. Years later when I heard this statement again I just shook my head.

I went to advanced infantry training (AIT) at Ft. Polk. Most of my company was Black and Hispanic. One Hispanic from Texas was in my squad. His nickname when translated into English was Pumpkin Head. We became friends and I was soon on very good terms with most of the Texicans. I found out that they were very loyal to their friends. This helped me survive in a somewhat dangerous setting in the nearby town of Leesville. The soldiers of Ft. Polk frequently called it Diseaseville; it wasn't much of a town. They still sold mule collars in the local hardware store at a time when Iowa farmers were starting to drive giant tractors with air conditioning. All of this was an education for an Iowa farm boy raised in a virtual all white community.

I was a squad leader all the way though the course. The reality was that we were being trained for a job with a mission. The mission of an infantryman is to "close with and kill the enemy." Nobody asked our commanding officers how close we had to get. Across the Pacific, some Vietnamese guy named Vinh was probably doing the same.

Once a soldier made a comment to an instructor about the danger of getting wounded. The instructor opened his fatigue top and showed the scars of at least five bullet holes. It didn't sound possible that anyone with five bullet holes would survive let alone still be able to work for the military, yet we were told medical attention in Viet Nam was quick and thorough. We would only be twenty minutes away from the hospital.

Near the end of training, I was asked if I wanted to apply for Non-Commissioned Officers or NCO school. I was selected to go to a program in infantry operations and intelligence. The training would guide us into command post positions with maps, pins, and so forth. At least that was the story being told to everyone. No third year of enlistment was needed for this program so I readily signed on. Trying to escape Uncle Sam's cold grip was harder than expected.

Chapter 6

REALITY SETS IN

NCOC School at the Ft. Benning, GA Infantry School was really an abbreviated OCS. We had many of the same instructors and classes. We were being trained to be Sergeants (NCOs) rather than officers. A lot of our infantry operations and intelligence classes were on map reading and other command post work. The map we frequently used was titled "Hue" because it was the principle town on the map. I didn't know it then, but I would use this same map many times in the Republic of Viet Nam.

Other companies in the area were being taught more advanced infantry. They would end up being squad leaders and platoon Sergeants in rifle companies. Others were being trained to be Sergeants in mortar platoons. The Infantry and Intelligence course was mostly designed to train men to work in map rooms and collect intelligence data. At the very end of the MOS job description was the one word that didn't look too important at the time: "**RECONNAISSANCE.**"

Ft. Benning in the Columbus, GA area was a welcomed break from Basic Training and AIT. We had most weekends off and could run around in civilian clothes on weekends. Many guys even brought their cars. About three weeks after arriving at

16

Ft. Benning, I received a letter from Donald Sparks. It was in his usual upbeat fashion. With his imagination, he had fashioned the Army into just another adventure. Not much was said except that he had just arrived at Nam and was in the 196th Light Infantry Brigade near Chu Lai. We had been exchanging letters about once a month. So far the Army had done him no favors. For a time he couldn't even walk from boot camp related injuries. Now he was in Nam as was his older brother, Ron. This was also not supposed to happen. Only one son per family was to be in Vietnam at one time. I sent him a letter telling him to end this war as soon as possible or I would be there in six months fighting in it.

In late June, my mother sent a letter saying that Don was missing in action. He had been in South Viet Nam for three weeks. I was in the chow line reading the letter. The news was devastating. I left the chow line and went back to the barracks. Up to that time the Army had just been another game to play. I became withdrawn and lost a lot of the spirit that had served me well in basic and AIT. This was no longer a game. My "old world" was gone and the news didn't show much promise. With a poor attitude, I somehow managed to finish NCO school. I still wonder if some North Vietnamese interpreter read my last letter to Don.

During my time at NCO school, we got into a mental tug-of-war with some Airborne Rangers that were supposed to teach us how to lead soldiers in physical training. They began acting like bullies. We were not allowed to shake the sand off our hands before going to the next exercise, which meant that sand would get on our necks and into our fatigue tops. One day we just sat down and refused to play these games.

Another time a man named Ken Burbank was asked to demonstrate how to properly do a push-up. What the Rangers didn't know was that he had reached the limit of toleration. The Rangers finally got upset when he tried to convince them that the angle of the back from the plane of the field should be exactly 15.5 degrees. He then went on with some more good techniques on the perfect push-up.

We got some terrible ratings and our Commanding Officer, or CO, was upset. Apparently the Rangers told him we were out of shape and soft. He decided to take us running but he had been back from Nam for too many months. He spent too many hours exercising his wrist at the officer's club. All went well for about a mile until the CO started to sweat. Soon he dropped out, and we kept on running for a few miles singing all the way. He later addressed us and said that it was obvious we were in shape. He was soon told about our beef with the Rangers. I was never able to stay away from Airborne Rangers even in Nam. I should have recognized that Ken's courage in standing up to others would lead him into a very elite group. On Aug 28th, 1970 he won the *Army Distinguished Service Cross* for actions above and beyond the call of duty.

We also got in trouble in other ways. Whenever an instructor told us something very irritating we would count out 46, 47, 48, 49, F**K YOU! This didn't go over too well, but they learned to tolerate us. Apparently the sheepish OCS guys never did this to the instructors. On our last outdoor training session for some reason, we were all in high spirits. There was a story going around that some of NCOC classes, including ours, were going to Korea instead of Nam. We went through the exercise screaming and having a great time, which was almost unheard of in the Army. Later that evening, a general addressed us and told us that the rumor about Korea was false. He told us that we were all going to Viet Nam. He got the obscene countdown and really lost it. I'm sure he took a personal interest in making sure our next duty station was indeed Viet Nam. I am not sure, but this probably was the same General who was second in command of the 101st Airborne Division the year I was in Nam.

Another incident happened while in NCO school. Two of our training Sergeants were Veterans of Nam. One day they disappeared. Word soon got out that accusations had been made against them about a massacre in a village called Mai Lai. They were both sent to live in a National Guard unit visiting from Puerto Rico the rest of the summer. This was in the summer of 1969 when the US public had yet to hear about this stain on

American history. A handful of undisciplined rogues destroyed the reputation of millions of decent men serving their country. Their photos were even deleted from the training company yearbook.

Chapter 7

TROUBLEMAKERS

The captain of our company was in a good mood, but in a bind. He ordered us to go down to the Sand Hill enlisted men's club and sell some sort of tickets he had to unload. A good part of the company with true altruistic spirit went down to sell the tickets. We had a great time and even sold a few tickets. There was a middle aged lady at the bar and soon word got to all of us that she was Airborne Annie, a woman that had lost three paratrooper husbands in Vietnam. I think she downed at least a dozen free drinks from the guys in a couple of hours while some of them stuck around listening to her stories and heartbreaks. Nobody proposed marriage to her and somehow everyone made it back before lights out. I will never know if she was the saddest woman in the USA or the best con artist in Georgia.

There were a group of troublemakers in the training company that loved to start rumors. They even called themselves rumor control. One day they almost brought Ft. Benning to a halt. There had been tension between the USSR and People's Republic of China for a few years. "Rumor Control" started a rumor that a hot war had broken out between the two countries. Soon discussion was centered on which side our government would ally with and send troops to. We all knew the Vietnam War was over if the two Asian Communist superpowers were putting their energies into fighting each other. The stories kept getting bigger and bigger. Finally the word came down to get back to work and that the stories going around were fabricated. "Rumor Control" had finally pulled off a good one. It broke up the monotony of one hot day in the Georgia summer. Nobody jumped on any big stories again.

We had finished up a training session on a very hot day; trucks came to give us a ride back to the barracks. The truck that my Platoon boarded was different than the nest. The side canvasses were down and roped shut. It was about a 120° inside with no breeze. We asked the driver if he would roll up the sides like the other trucks. He made a snotty remark that he would then have to roll them back down at the end of the day. Within seconds, bayonets were drawn and vent holes were cut in the canvass. He screamed that he would get in big trouble when he returned the truck. We didn't care. I met a lot of guys like him in the Army. In Nam, they were even worse. The driver had an easy job and would never go to Nam and he still felt sorry for himself having to do such minor work.

Soon we had a choice of where our on-the-job training would take place. One of the options was to go through Paratrooper school or even combine it with Ranger school at Ft. Benning. Jump school appealed to me because it was only three weeks long and I was getting tired of schools. There was also a lot of positive camaraderie among Airborne. Ranger school was quite a commitment. A couple of men took both Airborne and Ranger school. They had an angle. After finishing both schools they would have less than one year left in the Army. That meant the tour in Nam would be less than the normal one year. I have always wondered what became of those guys. I never saw any of them in Nam.

I decided against jump school because the second part of my on-the-job training would take place at Ft. Benning or Ft. Bragg. I was tired of the Southland by then. Ft. Carson, Colorado seemed a good choice for the three months of OJT. The two-week Recondo School in the Colorado Rockies also sounded good. To this day I have regretted not going to jump school.

Chapter 8

CARSON COWBOYS

I arrived at Ft. Carson on a Friday with no processing to be done until Monday. We were told that we had to stay at the welcome center and couldn't leave the post. Opportunity came in the form of a USO sponsored trip to Denver to an amusement park on Saturday. A group of us decided to take the trip. We stayed an hour or so at the park and got bored so we slipped out of the park and went out to see Denver. We missed the bus back on Saturday and checked out the nightlife of a western city. We caught another bus back late the next afternoon and nobody ever missed us. I was AWOL several times in the Army and was never missed.

Two of the guys who we had linked up with had just returned from Nam. They befriended us when we told them that we were scheduled to go in three months. They gave us a lot of encouragement. They mostly told us not to be a damn hero and charge the machine guns. From later experience, I must not have listened too well. I also had noticed that the real combat veterans rarely talked much about the glories of combat unless inebriated. That was reserved for others.

At Ft. Carson, I was assigned to a Battalion headquarters company in the operations and intelligence section (S2 and S3). Two Korean War-era Sergeants were doing most of the work. One of them liked showing off the Chinese Christmas cards that he found one morning outside his foxhole years before. I shared a room with a Cherokee Indian from Oklahoma named Carney. He had been in the 101st Airborne 1st Brigade in Viet Nam and talked a lot with me about "The Nam." He had a lot of pride in the 101st Airborne. I had no idea what the future would bring so I listened well. He had a great deal of respect for the enemy.

Our barracks room, with a nice view of Cheyenne Mountain and NORAD, was at ground zero if WWIII broke out. Carson on the surface seemed like a great place, but it was also a dangerous place. An information campaign was in place warning guys not to walk alone at night. I never saw any trouble, but Carney was rolled while hitchhiking back from Colorado Springs one night. The springs (Colorado and Manitou), as most called it, were wild places at night. Several of us would go to a local dive called The Hogan, which was off limits to military personnel. Ironically, most of the patrons were servicemen. It was a tough-guy place, but actually had few fights.

One night a young Lance Corporal Marine right out of Basic Training was sitting there all night in full dress uniform with a black leather glove on his right fist waiting for someone to insult the Marine Corps. We all waited around for the show, but nothing ever happened. Apparently everybody felt sorry for him, as there were plenty of guys around that could easily have ruffled his uniform. Some men even bought him drinks until he mellowed out.

There were a lot of urban cowboys in the place. Cowboy hats, jeans, boots and personalized belts were the normal attire. I used to talk to them about cattle ranching. It was a lot of fun playing games with them, as most of them were off-duty soldiers that probably only knew which end was the front of a cow. One of them got upset with me when I asked him too many pointed questions on animal husbandry, and I had to back off a little.

Guards routinely patrolled the parking lot by the Ft. Carson barracks with baseball bats at night. They were guarding the cars from being tampered with or stolen. They started using ball bats because empty M-14s were not any better and some guards had actually been rolled for their empty rifles. Once at Ft. Polk, I had to guard a huge warehouse with an empty M16. Basic lack of logic was the problem. A baseball bat was indeed better than an M16 that didn't work. I later saw that this was true in Nam also.

We were asked one day if we wanted to go to Recondo School. Everyone thought that it was required, not an option. I would have gone, but it required a shaven head again just like Basic Training. How could I go to town that way? Most days were spent doing odd jobs in the Intelligence and Operations section of the Battalion Headquarters Company. I ended up being the Battalion resident artist along with many other jobs.

The most boring job was updating Army field manuals. We would often adlib what we were working on. The Army has three types of salad dressings: oil, vinegar, and a combination of both. The old 'Sarges' would grin and bare it. Two guys from the BN did go to Recondo School. They both had gotten into trouble in Nam in the newly emerging drug culture and hoped to revive their military career by doing well in this school. After they were safely at the Recondo School we were told that it was unlikely going to help their career.

Chapter 9

LOVE MANEUVERS AND
FIELD MANEUVERS

I soon had a girlfriend in Colorado Springs. One night at The Hogan she ordered a flaming drink called a volcano. Soon she spilled it all over herself and was on fire. The police were soon there, and she was taken to a hospital. I was worried that the MPs would be there soon, but luckily enough people saw her spill the drink on herself. This gal was trouble and I tried to get her out of my life. She bothered me with phone calls and later wrote letters to me months after I was in Nam.

A week later I was with a few guys up in Denver and I met a girl from the Twin Cities, who worked for an airline company. Despite my vow a year and a half earlier not to get involved while in the military, I was smitten. We planned to get together again before I went to Nam.

Most weekends, a bunch of us would go sightseeing in the Colorado Rockies. We visited the Air Force Academy. I was awed by all the names of graduates that had died in Vietnam in the air war. This was the same area that my Uncle Donald Bock had trained in B-24s during WWII. It was like being on vacation just before going to the worst job in the world.

Our unit was on a big field maneuver south of Ft. Carson. The Army's 5th Mechanized Division's 2nd and 3rd Brigades were in obvious poor condition. The 1st Brigade was by the imaginary DMZ in Nam. Quite a few tanks and armored personnel carriers broke down within a few miles. One breakdown was interesting. Someone had replaced a petcock on an Army personnel carrier (APC) with a grease zerk. It soon lost all of its radiator fluid. Coincidence? I think not.

There was a parachute jump on the reservation that week. Two paratroopers landed against the side of a mountain and perished. I also viewed what barbed wired could do to tangle up a tracked vehicle.

The temperature was in the high 80s on the way out to the "war games" area. We had squirreled quite a few cases of beer in the Colonel's mobile command post. Most of the other rigs were searched before leaving. The first night we moved our cots out of eyesight up on a ridge and started enjoying our beer. Major Maury Finchum, one of the better officers I met in the Army, soon came up and caught us. "Be sure and bury all the cans when you're done" he said. He obviously was jealous that he couldn't be an enlisted man like the rest of us. He wouldn't join us. It was just too obvious what we were up to. The Army didn't want a bunch of DUI guys driving APCs and M-60 tanks, but they could tolerate a few beers after hours.

After a week in the field a blizzard hit. We were all caught off guard and no one had brought along heavy winter gear. One could only drive the APCs for half an hour before being frozen. I soon got my turn to drive. The control levers were identical to that of a bulldozer, which I knew how to handle. It was a lot of fun to drive an APC in the snow of the Colorado Rockies. Bulldozers don't move nearly as fast as an APC. I did skid out once. It was fun sliding it around curves in the road. At the time, all I could do was act my age, and I did.

27

Chapter 10

THE UNKNOWN AWAITS

One time a company in our BN was put on alert. They got their battle gear together and were preparing to ship out to an unknown location. Since I was in the S2/S3 shop I knew that they were on call because some college campus was acting up. This was something new to me, as soldiers had never shown up at Iowa State while I was there to maintain order. As it turned out the company sat around in front of the barracks for a while and never went anywhere. I believe most of them would have rather gone to Nam than go into combat against people of their own country.

One week in November papers came down for me to go for a physical workup. I was given some unusual vaccines including a smallpox vaccination that made me sick. I was sent to a two-day orientation school to get me ready for Nam. A couple of jackasses were there in boonie hats telling everyone that this would be their second tour and telling war stories. They nauseated everyone. My roommate Carney later told me in his stoic Indian style that they sounded like a couple of rear echelon types. Years later these types were still a bane to the good name of combat grunts. True combat veterans rarely talked that way.

A few days later I signed a million papers and went home on leave. Iowa was starting to get cold, but this was the winter that I would miss. I went to Iowa City to see my brother Stan. He was managing a place called the Red Ram. One of the employees in the place heard that I was going to Nam and was bound and determined that I should desert. It didn't take long to figure out that he was not that political, but a coward. If he really did believe all that leftist drivel, why didn't he just go and fight in uncle Ho's Army? He then told me that I was basically an idiot for going. He may have been right on that one.

I must have visited all of my extended family on this last leave before Nam. A family member gave me a nice St. Christopher's medal. He was the patron Saint of travelers. I still have it, even though the jungle stained it in a strange way. Even in the dark, light still flickers.

My last morning at home was very tense and somber. My parents could hardly say anything at all. Dad took me down to Des Moines. I don't think my mother was able to come along. She had once said goodbye to her two brothers closest to her in age and neither returned.

I left home a day early in order to visit Jeanne in Minnesota. Although it was only the second time we had met in person, Jeanne and I had been writing almost daily for two months. We had many long talks that weekend. She even hinted taking me to Canada. The lifestyle of a deserter seemed worse than that of going to Nam. After a very emotional farewell at the airport, I was on my way to Oakland Army base. Jeannie was almost in tears. The last days of the innocence in my life were coming to an end.

Since there was a time difference, I arrived in Oakland not much later than I left. I wasn't off the plane five minutes when two of my Texan friends from advanced infantry training came down an escalator. We had a reunion right there. They told me the "bush" was bad and that they had extended three years to get out of the jungle. They would have to go back and finish their tour in Nam, but would have rear echelon jobs. I would see this scenario again and again. It was a perverse way of filling the ranks of the Army. These guys just traded three more years of their lives to avoid six months of the bush. Who knows, it might have saved their lives. Was it really that bad, I asked myself? It was about 9:00 p.m. and I found a place in the airport that servicemen could flop for fifty cents on a military-like cot. I didn't want to check into the Army one day early. That would be idiotic.

After getting my gear checked in I did a little walking around the airport and tried to call one of my aunts that lived in Oakland. She wasn't in and I killed some time in one of those take your own picture booths. It was then I realized how lonely I was. On the way back to the bunk area, a guy motioned me over to him and gave me a cock and bull story and tried to lure me back to his apartment. He was obviously a homosexual doing a little fishing. I was in a different part of the country all right.

My last night in the USA was on a terrible cot in an airport USO area. I should have gone down to a good hotel with better room service. A few weeks later I would have done anything for that hard but dry cot.

The next day after a little sightseeing I went over to the Army base. There really wasn't much processing to do. I did get rebuked for not bringing my field jacket with me, but they gave me another. Who would need cold weather gear in the tropics? As it turned out the replacement field jacket was taken away from me in Nam. Ours was not to reason why certain things were done. We were scheduled to leave at 4:00 a.m. the next morning. I ran into a lot of guys from my NCOC school class. We were all on the same time schedule.

The trip over was very uneventful. We left with the rising sun and almost 24 hours later arrived with the setting sun. In the early part of the Vietnam War, guys that went to Nam went by ship or military air transport. We went by chartered airline. All the stewardesses were friendly, attractive girls from northern European countries. What a send off. Too bad none of them were kissing guys in the back row. We were treated very nice, but no cocktails.

Most of the guys were very somber. A few were going over for the second or third time. There was a long stopover in Hawaii. We were not allowed to do anything except walk around a small part of the airport. I was able to see my first 747 and get some sunshine. I did not experience sunshine again for a few months.

PART TWO:

VIETNAM

Highway 1 by Ocean south of Hue
(Photo courtesy of Terrance Downey)

Chapter 11

WELCOMING

We landed at a military airport in Bien Hoa, near Saigon. We sat around for several hours. The country smelled very different from the States. A green school bus, with chicken wire over the windows to keep grenades out, soon drove us through the area. We could see the sleazy nightclubs. As bad as it looked, I was told Saigon was safer than Chicago at the time. We were taken to some barracks, but sat around on the dry dusty ground for hours until they finally let us into them.

Sometime in the early morning, a very loud explosion went off about two blocks away. Sirens went off and vehicles sped around. Flares were sent up in the night sky and soon some small arms fire was heard in the distance. Some wise guy yells in a loud voice, "Welcome to Viet Nam." Soldiers with M16 rifles were immediately at each end of the barracks to protect all of us unarmed guys. Later we were told a VC sapper had sneaked in and blown up an F-101.

We went to a processing center for about one week. There was a signpost in the area that had all the distances to the major cities of the world and in which direction. Someone must have had some time to kill as it probably took a little research to put together. Very little processing was done. A lot of work was done by all of us. Some of us got to lead work crews of Vietnamese civilians. One very young pregnant woman was in a crew that I had to lead. I gave her a lot of slack because of her extended condition and she made some comment to the effect that she hoped her husband would not kill me. Apparently her husband was a VC. He was still out there somewhere.

My friend William Wong and I had been together in NCO school and at Ft. Carson. He was put in charge of a work crew also. One Vietnamese man kept staring at him and finally came up and pointed a finger into his chest. He said one word, "Chink!" William grinned and bared it. There was no Asian solidarity during this war. Vietnamese usually saw Chinese as an unwanted minority.

After one week we were all brought to a courtyard and lined up. I was selected to go to a place called Phu Bai, a place I never heard of. I was then unofficially told that I was going into the 101st Airborne Division at Phu Bai, which was just south of Hue (pronounced "**WAY**"). I had heard of Hue throughout the spring of 1968 and about the famous Tet offensive battle fought by the Marines there. It was also the scene of the greatest atrocity of the war. *The VC and NVA executed more than 4,000 people from Hue.*

I wasn't parachute qualified, but I was told they had a jump school in Nam. The guy didn't know what he was talking about. I caught a C-131 up to Da Nang and then took a CH-47 (sh*thook) up to Camp Evans just north of Hue.

The destination was called SERTs at Camp Evans. I believe this stood for Screaming Eagle Replacement and Training. The "Screaming Eagle" nickname goes back to WWII. The Vietnamese translated it as "Clucking Chicken" as Viet Nam did not have bald eagles and thought the Division symbol was a white chicken. Some other US military units called it the "Puking Buzzard" or the "1-0-worst." The 101st Airborne indoctrination was soon started.

We were told the 101st Airborne was the most feared US unit in Vietnam. I'm sure a few Marines disagreed. I knew that the 101st was involved in a battle the GIs called Hamburger Hill

35

six months earlier. We were given a few days of in-country training and a few days of familiarization with standard operating procedures.

In the northern part of the Republic of Viet Nam, the monsoons started in the fall and slowly died out in the winter. This is somewhat backwards from down in the Saigon area because there wasn't any dry ground to sit on. At least the bunkers had roofs. During in-country training the M-79 grenade launcher was discussed. I got into a disagreement with one of the instructors about its effectiveness. I would later see just how effective they could be in the wrong hands.

At a certain time, I had to check out an M16 for a training session. One of the two pins that held it together was broken so I went to an office after cleaning it and took a small piece of cellophane tape to hold the pin in so it would not get lost. When I went to turn it in, the L.T. in charge at the armory was trying to impress everyone on proper cleaning of weapons. When he saw the tape on the 16 that I turned in, he went ballistic instead of asking why it was on the M16. I calmly told him about the loose pin and walked away. He made a fool of himself in front of thirty guys. Officers and enlisted men that had trouble in the field were often given duty such as this L.T.

While on bunker line duty, we were told again and again not to panic when you see movement. Vietnamese farmers would bring their water buffaloes up to the perimeter at night hoping some green guy will blow them away. The reason for this was that the US government reimbursed the farmers $75.00 for each water buffalo accidentally killed. Raising buffalo to be shot must have been a lucrative business for the Vietnamese. I got to use a large night vision (Starlight) scope in the bunker, but it didn't work very well in the rain. No buffalo were killed on my watch.

Chapter 12

THE PEOPLE OF VIET NAM

The Vietnamese farmers I saw were incredibly strong. I saw one of them carrying firewood on his shoulders. The load was balanced over the body and must have weighed twice as much as the man carrying it. Instead of walking with the load, he was running right down highway 1, the only paved road in Nam. He was dodging 1950s era American automobiles as well as military trucks.

The women of all ages wore black pajama bottoms with white blouses. Young children went with no bottoms and were carried on the hip until they were ready to relieve themselves. Both genders wore a woven conical straw hat that was often covered with plastic wrap to keep out the rain. Only prostitutes would wear western skirts. I only saw one overweight Vietnamese woman during my whole tour.

The favorite vehicle of a Vietnamese family was a Honda motorcycle. It was not unusual to see a family of five on one. Another common vehicle was a little three-wheeled Italian scooter-like rig called a Lambretta used as a taxi. Twenty people would hang onto one of these. People picked through American garbage for food and anything else they could get a hold of.

Heavy corrugated cardboard could make a nice part of a shack for a few months.

One day a truckload of Vietnamese traveled to the firebase that I was staying at supposedly to do some contract work. Salvaging from the FSB dump was also part of their trip. They were actually better merchants than workers. Soon they had re-supplied many of the potheads with the devil's weed. It soon got worse. One of the line companies was just in from the field and quite a few were taking a long overdue shower. Soon several of the girl workers shed their black pajamas and went in with the guys. Their mission wasn't to get clean. This was international good will at its best. Not all the guys in the showers really wanted whores bothering them when they just wanted to get clean. The brass wasn't too happy about the so-called working women. During war times, no matter who you were, you had to be resourceful and strong in order to survive from one day to the next. Many of these people lived in shantytowns because of VC and NVA activity. Their own government, under a pacification program, resettled some.

Chapter 13

CONNECTIONS TO A
PROUD HISTORY

At Camp Evans, I found out that the 101st Airborne was not using parachute-qualified soldiers. It was now an airmobile division using helicopters. A year earlier, it had been called the 101st Air Cavalry. Now it was the 101st Airborne (Airmobile) Division. Jump school in Nam would have been good as it would have been another adventure to keep me out of the field for a few weeks. There is a strong brotherhood among paratroopers that is very positive, but parachutes weren't too practical in triple canopy jungle. A few weeks later, I would go to rappelling school instead.

Rappelling practice

Just before we left Evans we were divided by religion for services. I attended Catholic Mass in an old building. We were all given general absolution for our sins. A general absolution just before going home would probably have been more appropriate. During the rest of my tour, I would get a chance only one more time to attend Mass. Another time I attended an ecumenical/Protestant like service. Religion was apparently not encouraged. The mission statement of "closing with and killing the enemy" was apparently not in the Bible.

Finally after about one week at Evans I was put on a deuce-and-a-half truck and driven to Camp Eagle. I went with three guys I knew from NCO school in Ft. Benning. We drove through the old city of Hue and saw the damages made by the Citadel during the Tet offensive. One bridge had chunks of metal blown away from its I-beams and Army of the Republic of Viet Nam or ARVNs, as we called them, were guarding both ends. Many signs were in French and I never studied French so what I thought was a lingerie shop I found out years later was really a restaurant. On the road from Phu Bai to Camp Eagle some little children came running by the truck yelling, "Marijuana! Marijuana!" My jaw hit the floor from what I heard. Later on, I would hear worse from the children.

View from bunker line, Camp Eagle

Camp Eagle was just southwest of Hue and due west of Phu Bai. It was in the coastal grasslands. Leading west from it was a dirt road that went west toward Laos, which wasn't that far. Just southeast was a large flat hill, which was a good landmark for finding the base from the air. The camp was named after the symbol of the 101st Old Abe the Screaming Eagle. Years later in the *first Gulf War* there would be a Camp Eagle II in Kuwait. It is ironic how history somehow repeats itself.

We were all going to Company E 2nd Battalion 502 Infantry Regiment. Regiments weren't used in Nam by 1969. The 2/502 BN was part of the 1st Brigade along with the 1/327 and 2/327 BNs. The BN shield was an eagle's claw with the word "Strike" under it. We called ourselves "Strike Force" or more informally "The Five O Deuce." In WWII, it was once even called the O Duck. Another name from the Regimental days was Widowmakers. The pocket patch, which was rarely used, was a skull with bat wings. The WWII guys were apparently just as crazy as us Nam guys. In WWII, the 502nd parachute infantry regiment was divided as follows: 1/502 Companies A, B, and C; 2/502 companies D, E, and F and so on and so forth.

In Viet Nam after late 1967, each BN started out with a HHC or headquarters company and companies A (Alpha), B (Bravo), C (Charlie), D (Delta), and E (Echo). A, B, C, and D were line companies of three platoons each. E company included 90mm recoilless rifles, Mortar, Radar, and Reconnaissance or Recon Platoon. Company E had once been part of HHC, but it was separated a few years before. It was once called the Recondo Platoon while part of HHC. The Recon Platoon was led by a senior 1st L.T. and reported directly to the BN Colonel. The line companies all had a Captain and each of its three Platoons an L.T.

I was assigned to the Recon Platoon. After all, my MOS said that I was trained for such duty. They apparently thought that everyone that went to Ft. Carson had been to Recondo School. It wasn't worth mentioning this oversight to anyone. While I was with Recon, all the L.T.s were Airborne Rangers. I don't remember telling any of them the antics that occurred at Ft. Benning.

41

Since 1965 the mission of the Recon Platoon had changed. They were originally a heavily armed small unit that carried several M-60 machine guns. Recondo, as they were called then, was a combination of reconnaissance and commando. They were the first to go into an area before the line companies came in. They wore black berets and carried hatchets. They looked mean. The mission had changed over the years. They still went into an area first, but it was with stealth, not firepower. Ragged looking boonie hats had replaced the black berets, which were later reserved for Army Rangers. We were the only ones in the BN that wore full woodland camouflage. We snooped around and left no trace. All waste was discreetly buried. We were supposed to be the eyes and ears of the BN. When we found the enemy, the line companies would do the hard work. That's what I was told anyway, but it seldom worked that way. Recondo-like training was still passed on, but only a few had been to a Recondo school stateside or in Nam. We were often still called Recondos. Whether this was proper or not, I don't know.

The 101st Airborne Division and the 2/502nd Infantry had a proud history going back to WWII. We could trace our history to the Normandy beaches, the Battle of the Bulge, Operation Market Garden, and even to Hitler's own roost in the Bavarian Alps. The 1st Brigade of the 101st Airborne had arrived in Viet Nam in the summer of 1965 and traveled all over Nam for three years before the rest of the Division arrived in late 1967. They already had almost five years of history in Viet Nam and we were constantly reminded of this.

Chapter 14

COMBAT READY

I got to the company area on December 23rd. A guy from E company issued me my equipment. I was given one special plastic bag to keep my personal stuff in. Included also was a Ziplock wallet with Old Abe, the Screaming Eagle on it. This is now a rare collector's item. The rest of the gear was food and equipment.

I was given a brand new M16 made by H & R in Worcester MA, seventeen magazines, and enough ammo to fill each with eighteen or nineteen cartridges. It was generally accepted in military training both stateside and in Nam that putting the full twenty cartridges in an M16 magazine would weaken the spring and cause weapon malfunction. I was also given four fragmentation grenades and two smoke grenades. The grenades and ammunition were attached to a web belt. I was given a poncho, poncho liner, and a nylon pullover nightshirt. All non-combat gear was placed in a backpack that could be jettisoned when in contact with the enemy. We wore camo jungle fatigues unlike the line companies that had only olive drab fatigues. Boonie hats were worn in lieu of helmets.

No color patches were worn in the bush, but most guys had one uniform with all the glory patches for the rear areas. Echo Company's Top Sergeant Childers told me to find a place in the big tent next to the office. Before I left, he encouraged me and told me that the Recon Platoon hadn't lost a man in almost two years. I got a bad feeling from this comment. Would the luck hold?

Most of the rear buildings were made of 4x8 sheets of plywood with an 18-inch screened gap at the top to let air circulate. Corrugated steel sufficed for a roof. Sand bags as high as the plywood surrounded all buildings in case of incoming rounds. Christmas day was a truce day and I spent all day in the tent reading books. Then two of my classmates from NCO school and I went up to the Brigade enlisted men's club for a while.

Things were peaceful, but Clarence, a black man from my NCOC class had to learn the Dap. It was similar to secret societies with multiple handshakes. Blacks did it when they greeted each other. It lasted forever. A white man having a beer with a black man and a Chinese man was probably a rare sight. Peer pressure in the rear made sure that it never happened again.

The next day I was led across the vale that separated the companies from the heliport or landing zone (LZ). The vale had a stage and screen where movies could be shown. Later a basketball court and boxing ring were put in. I met a boisterous guy in E company. He started telling me of his plans to set the record for fastest time walking across Death Valley, but I wasn't too interested as I had my own valley to walk.

I caught a quick ride by helicopter over to Firebase Rifle south of Camp Eagle. The mountains were to the west and the ocean to the east. It was an exciting view. The route was right over the area where many civilians had been murdered in early 1968 by the North Vietnamese Army and some local Viet Cong during the Tet offensive. The last major cache of bodies had been found only a few months before my arrival. The coastal area was a tropical grass and rice paddy. FSB Rifle was a few miles, or clicks as we called a kilometer, into the jungle that lay west of the coastal plain.

44

Chapter 15

IN THE JUNGLE,
THE MIGHTY JUNGLE

FSB Rifle was in the foothills of the mountains. Once in the jungle, there were no villages seen from the air. Rifle was on a hilltop surrounded by other jungle-covered hills. There was a meandering bucolic river flowing by a short distance away. The terrain was similar to that of the Ozarks or the mountains of New England. The firebase had a battery of 105mm howitzers and a 81mm mortar pit area. There were many other bunkers for the officers and NCOs quarters. An underground command post was next to the artillery. It was a little city with concertina razor blade wire all around the periphery. A short distance from the wire were rows of fighting bunkers and huts for the grunts that protected the firebase from North Vietnamese sappers carrying little chunks of TNT called satchel charges.

I arrived with two other guys that were to join up with Recon. We checked in with Sergeant James of Mortar Platoon. He gave us a place to hang our gear and sleep. Recon was due in from the field and we pulled bunker duty at night and did odd work if needed during the day. Soon we were all asked if we were juicers or heads. Certain hooches or sleeping bunkers were reserved for those that only smoked marijuana or dew as it was called at that time in Nam.

One of the two guys I came out with shot himself in the foot. He claimed it was an accident, but everyone knew better. The other guy that came out with me told me that he couldn't believe anyone could do that to himself just to get out of combat. Less than two months later he was dead and the guy with the foot problem was probably healing nicely in a clean hospital in Okinawa. Nam was never fair.

On the last day of 1969, the Recon Platoon walked off of FSB Rifle and into the jungle. I was their newest addition. Soon we were lost in the thick jungle going up and down the hills. I don't remember being scared, but I did think to myself, is this for real because there was no more practice. I thought that I had either been trained for or heard about everything. I had not yet met a "Wait-a-minute plant."

I remember ducking under a vine where something grabbed and stopped me dead cold. It was a 6-8 foot long fern-like plant leaf that had barbs on it like fishhooks and it caught me. I didn't want to look weak in front of these Recon guys so I tried to power myself away from it, but it was no use. Soon the guy behind me came up and whispered that I shouldn't fight the jungle. He told me just to back up and it worked and soon I was free. The vine had won the round and I had a few cuts on my side.

The helper was a nice guy who had only one week left in the field. I know now he was assigned to be my watchdog. Good units trained and watched over cherries. He later taught me a few other little tricks such as how to tie boot strings on the back of the boot in a square knot to keep the brush from catching the loops. Even retying a shoestring messed up a platoon's patrolling. We walked out about 1 click from Rifle and made camp. The next day was New Years Day and it was a truce day. I don't know how all of this was arranged. It didn't make much sense; these were the guys who broke the truce day on the Tet holiday in 1968. We sat around all day and were ordered not to make any offensive maneuvers. In mid afternoon, I went down with a squad to fill the Platoon's canteens in a nearby stream. We found a site by the steam that the enemy had used a day before. The small fish at the site were spoiled, but not rotten. They apparently knew we were near and dee dee-ed away. All this was reported to BN and one minute after midnight after the truce was over; they worked some nearby areas with artillery. The year 1970 had started. They were in no haste to make contact with us. We patrolled the area around Rifle for about a month.

Although we were an Airmobile Division, a lot of the movement was by leg. One time when I was first with Recon we were issued a couple of rubber rafts. I wasn't privy to what the mission was. We humped out into the jungle and came to one of the most beautiful rivers that I have ever seen. We patrolled one side of the river and then had three guys paddle across at an area where the currant wasn't too strong. Two went out as guards to protect the other side. We then loaded up the raft with our gear and stripped down and swam the raft across with our gear nice and dry inside. I suspect that we were on a training mission although maybe it was a way of sneaking up on some enemy stronghold without being spotted coming in with Hueys. It was a fun mission and I took a few nice photos. The Marines would have been proud of us.

Playing Marine — Amphibious Assault

Chapter 16

BONDING BROTHERS

During the month of January I was in a squad. It didn't take long to get close to most of the guys. In a short time a person could know everything about a man. You would know his hometown, his religion, and his lady's name. The bonding was close and is the number one reason why guys would look out for each other. One guy was having marriage problems. He had been on a tour to Korea, came back, and got into a fight with his wife. He immediately volunteered for Nam and his wife didn't argue. A few months later, his wife met a Marine and is promptly pregnant. He was really upset and the men gave him sympathy. She sent him a very polite letter asking for a divorce. He read it out loud to all of us. He replied with a letter written in his blood refusing a divorce. He wanted to make sure the kid was born illegitimate. We all knew there were two sides to this all too common story that happens to soldiers of all generations.

A similar thing happened to a guy a few months later. During a period of terrible combat, a guy in Recon got a radio message stating congratulations your wife just had a baby. I relayed the message to him. He was upset and said there had to be a mistake as he wasn't home nine months before. As it turned out the wrong pack number had been sent to me. The look on his face was priceless when I first gave him the correct message. Luckily nothing happened to the guy before it was straightened out. It's now probably part of his family lore.

My friend William Wong was with me a week or two in Recon when he was transferred over to head the radar section of Company E. There were several reasons for his getting this position. The number one reason was that there was a great fear that he would be blasted away by one of his fellow Americans. This may sound kind of silly on the surface, but it was a real fear. The guys in Recon would not have been the problem. What if Wong was walking point or on observation point and another American unit walked up?

That situation once happened with Nguyen Tri, our first Kit Carson scout. Tri was out on OP. He came crawling back whispering that GIs were coming toward us. An American quickly crawled forward and called our universal "Strike Force" challenge. Tri was visibly shaken. If he had cried "Strike Force," he probably would have been shot by an American point man. I don't know how often the enemy actually used ruses to lure American troops, but stories were imprinted from the first days in Basic Training. Communist soldiers were reported to have called Medics in order to lure American medics to their death. I personally never heard the enemy talk or yell although we often did toward them during firefights. None of this is of course printable and usually had something to do with Ho's sexual habits.

During most of early 1970, we shared FSB Rifle with a unit of the ARVNs 1st Division, the Republic of Viet Nam's finest division. The first contact between the two allied forces was food exchange. They were happy at first to exchange their rice and canned mackerel for our C-rations in about equal volumes. After a while, you couldn't get them to exchange anything. The problem was that some grunts were more than happy just to give away their surplus Charlie Rats, as they were sometimes called.

49

FSB Rifle

Socializing thrived in a friendly manner. One ARVN began to like us and soon was giving us rice wine and inviting guys to have some of his food. They would bring bantam chickens out to the base and slaughter them. I was raised on a farm and had helped butcher many chickens, so witnessing how the Vietnamese prepared their chicken was quite engaging for me to observe. Instead of chopping the heads off and letting the chicken jump around, the Vietnamese way was almost ritual-like. Every feather was taken off the neck and then the neck was stretched out. This was a two-man job. A very precise cut was made in the neck and all the blood collected in a cup that was later used in the cooking. I never partook of the food, but did try some of the wine, which tasted like sake, Japanese liquor.

At a particular time, this same ARVN had a dark colored bottle of liquor. I probably would have taken some of it, but one of the guys asked why it was so dark. He told us in very good English that it was duck blood wine. I couldn't figure out if the man was joking around or not. After all the Spanish have a wine that means blood of the bull. So rather then trying some of his fine exotic wine, I politely declined his invitation. I was never offered any rice wine in the future.

Cultural gaps always exist, but in most cultures, refusing to drink or eat with someone is a social blunder. The ARVN was

50

very friendly and told how his family came from the north years before to escape from the Communist threat. Some of his relatives had died two years before when the Communists slaughtered thousands in the Hue area. He did not seem a rabid anti-Communist, but had no love for them either.

Overall the Americans and ARVNs worked fairly well together. Only a few incidents occurred that caused a little friction. The first involved ARVN jealousy of the electric power lines that were strung all though our hooches or bunkers. We didn't ask permission to go ahead with this and neither did the ARVNs. One night one of them sneaked over and ran a line over to his hooch. Unfortunately for him he shorted the thing out, and he got yelled at.

Another time one of our guys had the bolt of his rifle stolen. He perceived that an ARVN took it so he felt justified walking over in broad daylight and stealing the bolt of a random ARVN soldier when the soldier was gone. Apparently our American brother was seen taking it and all of Recon had to stand in a group for the witness to pick out the culprit. Our guilty man was indeed worried so we crowded him in the middle of the group. We all wore our boonie hats low on our faces. Clarence went with us even though the witness said that it was one of the white guys. Despite being the blondest and the most distinctive looking guy, he was not pulled out of the lineup. It proved that All-American guys appear alike no matter what race. Later the BN armorer gave the ARVN a bolt for his rifle.

Shortly after this happened, another prank took place, which was quite the meanest I had the honor of viewing in my whole life. Recon was given a case of WWII vintage pineapple grenades for the bunker line. We were all amazed that any were still around, but at any rate, one of the guys had a bright idea. He unscrewed the top off the grenade and pored out all the powdered TNT. Then he took the trigger and fuse-assembly and chucked it a safe distance so the cap wouldn't hurt anyone. When the grenade was put back together, it appeared just like the original. Later that day, an ARVN soldier walked into his little privy to do his business. The dummy grenade was then tossed in. Within seconds, the startled ARVN bolted out with his pants down around his ankles and then promptly tripped and fell flat on his face. This time there was no lineup. Our Platoon Leader L.T. Ciccolella gave us a little lecture about whose country this was and how the ARVNs were our allies, not enemies, but we all detected a slight grin on his face. They played some tricks back on us, but were never able to match the grenade prank. Those twenty-five-year old grenades worked, but we only used them around the firebase. I read years later how this trick was played in WWII and in Korea. Some things never change.

Chapter 17

SURVIVAL

We moved to a new area every day and never stayed at one location. If you were a noisy unit and stayed three nights in the same spot it could mean trouble real quick. The NVA would find a similar location and practice all day on attacking and overrunning your location. While taking stateside training, we were told that while patrolling we were to keep guys on the flanks. This was rarely done because the jungle was too thick. If a guy got out of sight on the flanks, he was in grave danger. Making a trail in the jungle also makes noise.

We kept distance, but not so far as to get separated. The patrol was led by a point man. This was probably the most dangerous place to be. The point man had to do many things at once. He had to watch for signs of the enemy. Footprints told him if he was on a used trail. The NVA frequently had trail watchers. They didn't always shoot. They might go back and alert the rest of their unit. Sometimes they set up a mini ambush and emptied a banana clip from their AK-47 and then ran away. They also left trail markers on trees. The point man also had to find trail and sometimes work his way through the underbrush. Plus, he had to watch for booby traps. The point man had only an

M16, which he kept on safety. The safety could be flicked off in a millisecond while diving for mother earth.

We once had a point man accidentally set off some rounds while walking with the selector on full automatic. He killed some brush and gave away our position. We had to quickly go in another direction. Working in conjunction with the point man was the slack man. He had to help the point man in any way he could. If the point man was working through brush he had to stay close and watch ahead to protect the point man. This teamwork would vary depending on the type of terrain and the situation. The rest of their squad, which included the squad leader, followed the point man and slack man. The squad leader's position could be the third man or back a little further in the column. He was usually guiding the point man as to which direction to travel. This was done by compass or dead reckoning using terrain features on the topography map. Hand signals were generally used. If anything needed to be verbalized, the squad leader would go up and talk to the point man while the slack man moved slightly ahead and watched. If the patrol was platoon sized then the platoon command post or CP followed the first squad. The CP consisted of the Platoon leader usually a 1st L.T. and the Platoon Sergeant usually a staff Sergeant. In addition, there might be one or two radiomen (RTOs) and sometimes an artillery forward observer (FO). The last two squads followed.

If a guy had to relieve himself, he stepped aside, did his duty, and then went back up to his spot in the patrol. When crossing an open area like a road or stream, guys in the column would one after the other watch the open area on each side until relieved by the next guy in the column. If the point man found the enemy then one squad could go to the left and the other to the right. The third squad would protect the rear and flanks. At least that's how it was supposed to work. Sometimes it went exactly like that. Other times it was confusion in the jungle for both sides.

The very last man was the tail or drag. His job was to keep watch in the rear to make sure the unit wasn't being followed. He sometimes sat down out of view for a little while, watched, and then hurried to catch up. It was dangerous to get

54

out of sight of the man ahead of you. If a drag man saw the enemy following, he could hurry up ahead and the squads could set up an ambush. I never saw this happen. A good unit would stay undetected.

This type of patrolling was dangerous if the enemy hit from the side. It was wise to minimize walking on established trails. The NVA didn't like breaking trail so they frequently had multiple routes to minimize using the same trail. You could find fresh footprints and wait for days before the trail was used again.

Our primary mission wasn't setting up ambushes. We did frequently stop and set up our night camp, or even stop for lunch on a trail. Usually this was right across a large trail. We sometimes called the large trails yellow brick roads. Small side trails were sometimes called dee dee trails after the Vietnamese word for getting the heck away.

When camping at night or during the day we always had observation posts (OPs) out a short distance in all directions especially on trails. At night Claymore mines were almost always set out. They were slabs of C4 explosive with 700 pea-sized ball bearings on the convex side. The convex side had the words "Front toward Enemy." The concave side had a nasty back blast so when they were set up close to our positions we liked to point them slightly up so the back blast would hit the earth. Officially, you were supposed to be back at least 16 meters, but this was rarely the case. One danger was that the enemy would sneak up and reverse them. Then he would go back, toss a small rock, or even show himself.

A Claymore mine detonated only three times while I was with Recon. One time a new guy either sat on the trigger (Clacker) or was holding it in his hand too tight. The other two times were during combat. Usually at night on OP, you left it lying in reach just in front of you. Several grenades were also placed in a row along with one or two extra M16 magazines. We sometimes used trip flares, which could be used safely very close to our positions, but they weren't perfect. One guy got burned taking a trip flare down one morning. We were never hit at night, which meant we did a good job of slipping into a night position.

When we were patrolling FSB Rifle Sgt. Hipp carried a body bag with him. This was unnerving, but the rationale for his action was that if a comrade was killed, the body could be put respectfully into the bag immediately. However the real reason was that the bag made a nice waterproof sleeping bag. Not everyone liked him humping this reminder of sudden death around with him. After the monsoons wound down, he left it in the rear. No one missed having it along.

Chapter 18

THE PRIMITIVE JUNGLE

When I arrived out in the field, the worst of the monsoon season was over. In the fall of 1969, a typhoon hit and the grunts had to sleep in the water. It still rained in January, which didn't matter too much during the day. Getting wet at night was no fun. We usually pitched very low two or three poncho tents. A whole squad could sleep under a three-poncho tent. We would cuddle up to each other for warmth in the order set up for guard duty. We all had a polyester sleeping shirt and a poncho liner. Body heat could dry both out if you first rung them out.

When I was growing up in Iowa I developed a sensitivity to corn. It was not good being allergic to the major crop of a state. After a few weeks in the jungle a skin rash developed that was driving me crazy. There was no way to wash it and secondary infections started. After a little experimentation, it became apparent that the flora responsible was bamboo. I went to the medical shack on FSB Rifle and they gave me some lotion. They talked a little about getting me out of the bush, but nothing came of it. A few weeks later another guy developed something similar, and he was given a jeep-driving job. I learned to avoid bamboo, which wasn't always possible. Later when we moved west of Hue into the high mountains no more bamboo was to be seen. Even today bamboo reminds me of the misery of those first few months.

While on guard duty I would leave the poncho-made tents in my poncho and set myself in an inconspicuous place by the claymore clacker and the row of grenades. In the tropics, days and nights are similar in length year round so we ate before dark and had long nights. One or two hours of guard duty didn't dip into sleep time too much. One of the favorite tricks was to put the new guy on last watch. A luminescent watch was passed down the line every hour. Somebody always seemed to move the watch ahead to get out of their guard duty. The squad leader would have to hold court in the morning to find out who cheated on watch. If it was a new guy that got the last watch the culprit could get away with it.

Making enemies was not a smart thing to do in a combat unit. The watch trick was highly frowned upon except with a new guy. You paid your dues when first joining a squad. I usually volunteered for last guard since I couldn't sleep for more than 8 hours. The early mornings in the jungle were neat. One time I had guard on a very dark night. Something was making a slight noise above me. An animal just barely discernable was slowly coming down a tree about 3 feet from me. When it got almost to the bottom, I reached over and lightly snapped my fingers. There was a hell of a commotion as it went back up the tree. It woke the Platoon Sergeant up, and he came over on his belly with his M16 to see what was going on. He was relieved when I whispered to him that it was just an animal. Just an animal! In the year I was in Nam two Marines had a tiger circle around their position one whole night. This was the jungle at night.

The command post or CP didn't have to pull guard except with the radios. RTOs slept with one ear by the radio in case a message came in. They would be in the center with three squads around them. This was not necessarily the safest place as officers, NCOs, FOs and RTOs were prime targets.

We were re-supplied every three days. Every man was given three days worth of C-rations and a few dehydrated meals called LRRPs after long-range reconnaissance patrol. C-Rations were canned and packaged food. Each was an individual meal. I believe there were twelve different kinds in each case. Each had a small can opener we called a P-38. Beer openers were commonly called B-52s. Nam era Charlie Rats were better than the K-Rations and C-Rations of WWII, but not as good as the modern MREs the military uses now. LRRPs were designed for the patrols that went into border areas for a week or longer and needed to keep backpack weight down. All you had to do was add boiling water. Some food was downright good and others marginal.

A lot of trading would go on as guys collected their favorite kinds. Old timers usually went first. Many care packages arrived and were passed around. Some were full of liquor. In addition to the Charlie Rats and LRRPs, we received a so-called "Sundry Pack." In it were toothbrushes, toothpaste, and other personal supplies. Multiple brands of cigarettes were included along with Red Man loose chewing tobacco. Included were a few treats such as tropical chocolate that wouldn't melt even on the hottest and most humid days. It was not Swiss chocolate, but it helped a sweet tooth survive. Trioxane tablets were used to cook over a miniature stove made from a tin can with holes in it. It elicited a nice cool blue flame like a gas range. A cookbook could have been written about some of the ingenious combinations cooked out in the jungle over a trioxane tablet.

The one thing that was sought after from home was hot sauce. It made even canned turkey or ham and eggs palatable. Nowadays, MREs have hot sauce in some meals. After a few months you could even tell by the label if the beef was going to be lean or gristly or if the canned pineapple was tender just by looking at the company name on the can. One supplier would use good beef and the next second rate. Anything for the troops! All this may sound very good until you have been in the jungle for months without a mess hall cooked meal. The canned ham and eggs C-Ration was by far the worst. The beans in the chili con carne LRRPs never became fully re-hydrated and were often crunchy. Only one time in my nine months in the jungle did they bother to bring a mess hall style meal in canisters to us on re-supply day.

The choppers would come in and dump off all the food, ammo, mail, and other supplies. About every other re-supply we would get a change of clothes. One time, we went over a month and the jungle fatigues started to rot off of us. Some guys had gaping holes in their fatigues. We never wore underwear so there was no secondary protection. Modesty wasn't the problem. Scratches and leeches were. The choppers would come back in a second time and pick up dirty clothes and some leftovers. Sometimes the L.T. would leave for a meeting and then come back. I would then get stuck selecting his food. I never got a complaint.

The leftover food was a problem. At first all cans had to be punctured. Later it was learned that this was not good enough as the gooks would come in and collect even these tins. We had to empty all cans out into a shell crater and mix with dirt and excreta. Then the mess was buried. Some units buried a grenade in the midst of the leftovers as a party favor. This was frowned upon. A grunt might excavate the same hole a year later and run into it. The rule was that if you set up a widow-maker as we called them, you had to take it down if it didn't go off. Other units would move out of a site and leave an ambush team behind. That worked for a while, then the surviving gooks would get smart.

Another reason we buried all leftovers was ravens. A flock of ravens working on a site would tell the enemy the area where you were patrolling. Part of the pacification program was to keep rice from getting into the hands of the VC and later the NVA. By 1970 the program was working well. They were frequently near starvation or bored with their diet of rice, rice, and still more rice. The NVA soldiers put a fermented dried fish powder called nuoc mam on their rice. Some grunts could smell it at a distance and warn the others. The enemy in turn probably could probably smell our fine American cigarettes.

Chapter 19

INDOCHINA CRITTERS

One of our best point men when I was first with Recon was a Northern Cheyenne Indian from Montana whom we affectionately called Chief.

Comrades Lloyd "Butch" Hume and
"Chief" Fenton Flying

One time we were walking as a platoon near FSB Rifle and Chief gave a stop signal. The slack man came up to help out. There was a slight conference between them, and the slack man

61

covered while Chief put his rifle down. He then picked up a good-sized rock and flung it at something on the trail. I think he did a slight war dance to entertain us. We all were wondering what was going on. The L.T. came up to the front with that look of bewilderment on his face. The whole column came up and made a small perimeter.

L.T. Ciccolella asked what was going on and was told that a python had been lying across the trail. Chief had obviously seen *Tarzan* movies where pythons grabbed animals or even humans that stepped over the top of them. The L.T. asked where it went and Chief pointed in the direction. We went over that way and found a large shell crater half filled with water. At the bottom of the crater was a crocodile looking up through the water with a bruised tail. Not much was whispered, but there were a lot of grins all around. Chief had this way of sneaking up on critters.

Another time there was a slight commotion up front, and word was sent back that some rock apes in the trees had tossed some feces at him. In the jungle, you get little respect. One time on patrol we came to an area that on first glance it appeared that the NVA had been dragging something big through the jungle. The under brush was flattened in one direction and a wide trail was made. We followed the trail for a distance until we hit a muddy place and could make out elephant tracks. It was another mild embarrassment for the point man. I would later "See the elephant" in a figurative way.

Cobras and other snakes were all over the place, but they were not aggressive. We stopped one noon with a line company. One of the guys from the company was writing a letter while leaning on a tree. I saw this very long snake slide right over his legs at a high speed. The guy jumped about 4 feet up. I once saw a very large snake in a state of decay, no doubt killed by some idiot. The war was probably very bad for wildlife. The tiger is probably extinct there now. Much of the wildlife was probably destroyed, although recently they found a new species of a deer-like animal in Indochina.

One morning I arose from a sound sleep and grabbed my boonie hat. When I put it on, something bit me on the cheek. I thought the worst, that it was a small snake. The culprit was stomped on and examined. It was an 8-inch long centipede. It was orange on top and a little lighter on the bottom about the same color as a cooked crab leg. Soon the stinging pain led to swelling. A few guys were giving me some grief about the whole thing. No one had ever heard of these things that like to make their homes in hats.

I went to Doc Ackerman and showed him my dead centipede and the swelling in my cheek. He talked to the Battalion aid station and they told him to watch me for a while. Soon the whole side of my head was swollen. Because of my condition the whole Platoon didn't move out at daybreak as planned. Just when it looked as if I was going to be choppered out, the swelling started to go down. I was given a lot more grief about doing anything to get out of the field. To this day I catch myself shaking out my shoes and looking in hats before putting them on.

Land leeches were the most miserable thing that grunts encountered in Nam. Most people think of leeches as things found in the water that swim to you and attach themselves, but in Nam, these little bloodsuckers live on land. They looked like cabbage worms inching along. The problem was they were always inching toward their next meal. Funny enough that meal was you.

If you stood in one spot you could see them coming from all directions toward you. When you moved a few feet away from your original position, they would in unison all change direction toward you again. When grunts were in bad leech country, they began to tuck their fatigue shirt into the trousers. Other little things helped. Elastic bands or shoelaces around the wrists, elbows, knees, and ankles helped. I once showed a photo of a grunt to a guy stateside and he thought the elastic band thing was a fashion thing among Nam guys in order to look macho.

Military insect repellant was hell on leeches. Just a small drop on a leech and they would turn white in color and die. Some guys hated them so much that they got pleasure out of torturing them with cigarettes. They would hit you 24 hours a day. It was not unusual to wake up in the morning and find a leach attached to some remote part of your body, like up the nose or on the crotch. It was not uncommon to see a guy walking along with blood streaks on his body where leeches had attached themselves. The bite site would bleed for about fifteen minutes.

They were silent workers and sometimes you didn't know one had been on you until it dropped off and you felt the weight change. Liberal use of bug repellant in addition to seamless uniforms helped. The group that designed jungle fatigues designed them for comfort and didn't think about leeches getting in the loose clothing. At night guys sometimes put salt or pepper circles around their sleeping position. Chief got a hold of some spray bug repellant and circled his sleeping spot. That seemed to work better than the seasonings. He was teased a little about learning the trick from his Northern Cheyenne ancestors and wagon trains.

One time we found a very nice mountain pool, and some guys decided to take a dip to clean off. They came out with some giant water leeches attached to their naked bodies. Jungle that had been defoliated grew back nasty bamboo, wait-a-minute vines, and other brush. It was also the worst leech country. Agent Orange must have helped them reproduce faster.

One of the guys in Delta Company had a pet monkey. I was surprised that the brass let him go out in the field with it. I suppose his chattering and screeches fit right into the camouflage of an infantry company. He would catch a ride with either his owner or another handy ride. Sometimes he would jump from one guy to another. I once had the honor of having lunch with Jo Jo and his master. He was a real pain getting into my food until he settled into that age-old monkey routine of attempting to groom parasites out of my hair. I heard later that Jo Jo couldn't get a permit to go back to the USA. I hope he didn't end up as wok meat over there.

The only other animals on the firebase were small lizards. They would come out on the brighter days to warm up. They made a very peculiar sound by filling themselves up with air and letting go a two-staged call. It was a combination that is frowned upon in polite society and sounded like this: F**k You! This wasn't a tall story. Most American guys, when they first heard this very loud comment by the geckos, would turn their head in shock. Some even thought fellow humans were doing it. The Vietnamese saw no humor in it, but in English it was funny hearing these lizards tell you off. I don't really need to say what we called these little bad mouths. I've read that there were versions farther south in Vietnam as large as cats.

Chapter 20

GIRLS AND GRUNTS

One of the line companies had to blow a tree to help make a landing zone. Claymore mines had two other uses other than killing the enemy. You could take out the C4 explosive and use it in place of Trioxane tablets to cook your supper. The C4 could also be used to blow trees. It was safest to take it out of the mine, but in an emergency the ball bearing side could be pointed toward the tree.

Some guy from the Line Company got lazy and didn't take the C4 out of the mine and then got stupid. The concave side of the mine fit nicely against the convex round tree. The problem was that the side of the mine that said "Front toward enemy" on it was pointed outward. When the clacker was pulled not only did the metal pellets go straight outward but they probably went out at a much faster velocity because the mine's back blast was against the tree. Several men were killed in this incident. This company killed more of its own for a long period of time than the enemy did. Even their ambushes often backfired and the NVA would sneak up on them. It was that way with them almost the whole time I was with the BN.

In January, the Army moved the whole 2/502 to a new area of operations, or AO. We were to sweep a large area and find a large NVA force and destroy it. Some officer came out and told us that everything was secret. He said that soldiers even went to some cathouse in Hue and gave false information to the girls. They in turn would most likely give the information to the NVA. I can just see some soldier saying that this is against his moral code, but he would do it for God and country.

Sgt. Hipp gave us a long pep talk before we started out. It sounded like we were really going to hit some bad stuff. We spread out and swept a large area near FSB Veghel. The area where FSB Veghel was located, west of Hue, had seen some terrible fighting two years before. The second day a guy from a line company was taking his turn watching a stream when a lone NVA soldier walked out into the stream to fill his canteen. The NVA was immediately shot and killed.

View of FSB Veghel from Hill 882

We were about 2 clicks (kilometers) away. One guy in Recon who had been in Nam three years came up to the L.T. and was begging him to get permission to go over and help. He said that maybe we can get us a gook or two in a Count Dracula accent. I took this as a lot of bravado to impress the other guys. I'm still not sure though. Late one afternoon we got terribly lost.

67

The L.T. had two airburst of artillery set off at the corners of two grid squares on the map and he triangulated our position by sound. Not knowing exactly where you were in the jungle was a very risky situation.

Luckily we soon linked up at our intended destination and all looked well. The great sweep was a failure. Almost no gooks had been killed. The girls had let us down. We would return to this area a few months later. The neighborhood would go downhill.

During the great walk, my feet started getting sore. We walked through a lot of water and despite multiple sock changes; I was never able to keep my feet dry. Soon there was a burning sensation in the soles of my feet. The whole bottom layer of skin sloughed of my feet just like skin on a snake. The next day my feet didn't get wet and soon the crisis was over. Most grunts kept two or three pairs of socks. Wet ones could be wrung out and dried by placing close to the chest or dangled from the backpack. The problem was that socks were getting wet faster than the spare socks could dry.

Chapter 21

LIVING THE AMERICAN LIFE
IN VIET NAM

I had by this time settled into the routine of being a rifleman in a squad. I had not made any errors and was getting along with the other guys. At the appropriate time, I felt ready to move up to squad leader. Near the end of the great walk an incident happened that would change this course.

Late in the afternoon, a chopper came in and brought in a new guy. As it turned out, he was new to me, but had been in Recon for months. He had just returned from training to be a squad leader. The first thing he did when he came to my squad was stand on my poncho liner that had just been set out for the night, and he wiped his feet. I rebuked him and told him to get off. My insolence really irritated the little Napoleon.

He had me transferred to his squad and was determined to break me. I just ignored him for the next few weeks. He was close to getting his reward when wiser people than him found a new place for me. We still would be in Recon together for months. He always tried to impress new people, but we just ignored each other and I went on to the platoon command post and became an RTO and FO. The only time he ever said anything in the future against me was when he complained during an on-line assault that my M16 was hurting his ears. He distracted me just enough to almost get us both killed.

Shortly after the big sweep, we spent a few days on a different firebase. An officer soon came around to inspect. He was extremely nervous and wanted to make sure the defenses were improved. It soon became obvious that something was wrong with him. He was excessively fearful and it showed. We were all wondering what was wrong with the guy. He told us to find some powdered lime and cover the soil around the hillside so it would be white. The idea was for us to see the enemy sappers crawling up better at night. It actually wasn't a bad idea, but the first rain would have made it disappear. Many other strange actions arose and soon he was relieved of his command. It was always sad to see a career officer or enlisted man perform wonderfully stateside and just totally lose it in a combat situation. Some men were great in the stateside Army, some only in combat. Others did well at both. They ended up at the top.

Once while stationed on a long-forgotten firebase I ran into what we called a Donut Dolly. Red Cross girls were frequently called Donut Dollies. Calling them a Donut Dolly was not a good way to get on their good side. They lived in what seemed like a paradise for women. There were hundreds of grunts that were always trying to get to know them better. We talked for a while and we found that both of us were from Iowa. We even had some mutual acquaintances back in the world I once knew. She had just finished college at Drake University. After a few minutes, she was off to talk with other guys or deliver a message or something. This was one of two times that I talked to American women in Nam. The next time it would be with nurses at a hospital.

Chapter 22

BEING RECONDO

One of the more interesting sideshows frequently seen in the jungle was the use of Air power. This came in several forms. Small light observation helicopters called Loaches (LOH) armed with mini guns would buzz around the jungle looking for targets of opportunity. They reminded me of fast moving hummingbirds.

When a mini gun was used the rounds came out so close together that it sounded like a continual loud burp. Sometimes pink teams or a duo of a Loach and its bigger cousin the Cobra would work together. The loach would work down low. When it got in trouble or found something the Cobra would go to work. Cobras used mini guns, but also used 40mm grenade launchers and air to ground rockets. A Cobra was a Huey with a slim body. It was fast and could cause a lot of havoc with enemy troops on the ground.

It was a lot of fun to watch cobras do their dives. I loved the chopping sound the rotors made when banking hard. The granddaddy of air support was the Air Force and its jets. They would come in and drop 500-pound bombs or barrels of napalm. I was always fascinated with how fast and low those Fly Boys would come in. Watching the bombs or barrels drop in at great speeds was quite a show. I believe it was the F101 that was sometimes called a "Thud," the sound they supposedly made upon impact on the ground. I remember quite a few times listening to some lonely dink clacking away with his AK at a Cobra or jet hoping to collect some military reward.

Air support was predicated on the pilots knowing exactly where friendly troops were located. We marked our location by use of smoke grenades. This worked well if you weren't in too deep a jungle and the wind wasn't blowing too hard. We had many different colors of smoke. The proper color had to be verified with the pilot before he let go his load. Purple was usually called grape, yellow was banana, etc. The clever enemy often popped smoke to confuse the pilot. Quite a few fatal miscalculations happened in Nam while using air support.

One day all of the Recondos went to rappelling school. Most of the old timers had been there before. Our personal equipment was a piece of rope and a metal clip we called a D-ring. Everyone in the Recon Platoon carried these two pieces of equipment at all times.

It was a lot simpler to set up than the fancy leather harnesses and multicolored carabineers used in what is now a sport. We learned how to wrap the rope around our legs and hips. No granny knots were tolerated. We then snapped on our D-ring. I did three successful rappels down the nice flat wood tower on a doubled up rope and it was easy.

The next time we trained, it was out of a hovering helicopter. This was much more difficult, but we all passed the ordeal. We would later use this technique in jungle insertions in areas where LZs had not been blasted yet. There was a high probability of death if an enemy soldier got close enough to shoot while you were sliding down from a hovering chopper in a hot LZ. If a chopper was fired upon while you were going down the rope the pilot might take off. You would then have a long dangling ride back to a safe area assuming you didn't fall off.

One day, the BN XO made a snide comment about Recon not killing a gook in a long time. A few days later we returned to the jungle around Rifle and went back to patrolling. We set up a noon perimeter and a squad went out to check an area that

72

intelligence had said was suspicious. They were gone for about an hour or so and came back in. One of the men from the returning patrol commented that there's nothing around there.

A few minutes later this stocky muscular gook walks right up to one of our OPs and one of our squad leaders stitches him with his M16. An automatic rifle can leave a trail of holes across a body. This happened within sight of me. I saw the guy fall with anguish on his face. Gooks had one fatal flaw when moving. They usually slung their AK-47s over their shoulders. It took too long a time to take it off and fire back. An AK is not a comfortable rifle to tote by hand. We didn't know if he was the point man of a large unit or a sole messenger.

Another possibility was that he had seen our patrol and was following it in order to locate our night defensive position. A combat perimeter was set up and the body stripped of anything that might be of use to Army intelligence. After a half an hour of silence, we slithered away.

The 502 Regiment, going back to WWII, was sometimes called the Widowmakers. One of the guys went over and left a calling card in the hand of the dead enemy. The card had the usual BN symbols and a message in Vietnamese. Translated, it read, "He went off to war to be a Viet Cong hero, now his wife's a widow, compliments of the Strike Force Widowmakers." These cards were illegal by the Geneva Convention, but the officers never bothered anyone using them. There seemed to be an endless supply of them. Other units in Nam left black scarves or the Ace of Spades. In 1965 the Recon's pocket patch was the Ace of Spades with an eagle's head in the middle. Aces over eights would have made more sense.

From an intelligence point of view, leaving a death card was extremely stupid. You were telling the enemy exactly who you were. The information could be passed on to their intelligence section. This was the first combat that I saw although I did not participate. Despite this contact and several others by line companies, the FSB Rifle area was considered a quiet area of operations or AO.

The line companies and Recon would occasionally get a turn at bunker-line duty around a firebase, but there was one advantage—a dry bunk (in what else? a bunker) was the reward. The bunkers had a wall of sandbags with some half culverts for roofs. The roof was sometimes sand bagged in case of mortar attack. What we had was a damp hole in the ground akin to a homesteader's dugout only smaller. A few feet away toward the bunker line was a fighting position of a foxhole with a double row of sandbags in front. There was the usual cache of grenades, M16 magazines, and clackers hooked to wires that ran down to claymore mines and buried drums of napalm with claymores under them. Trip flares were set up in the perimeter's concertina wire.

The Luxury Condo on FSB Rifle

At night we would take turns in the fighting positions. During the day we would work on the concertina wire perimeter or go on short patrols outside the wire. We would try and put trip flares in places that even an experienced sapper might set off. There was always a lot of work around the FSB, but at least during the day it was relatively safe. Mortar fire was always a concern, but the enemy was shy of using mortars during the day when light observation helicopters could find their tubes and direct cobra gun ships or even jets with bombs. We never got mortared at FSB Rifle. We even had a pet dog on the firebase. One of the guys had a Vietnamese yellow dog. They only had one breed of dog in the whole country. His name was Stud and he had a great life with a couple of hundred guys petting him. It's a miracle he wasn't eaten by the ARVNs.

Chapter 23

ROUGHING IT

There were no women on Rifle so relieving oneself was relatively easy. At regular intervals we positioned piss tubes. They were 4 inch round pipes going down into the ground. They were just high enough out of the ground at the top for the average guy to reach and relieve himself. We were not allowed to leak anywhere we wanted because military sanitation was supposedly at its finest. If squatting had to be done, we had an old fashioned privy. Only the waste didn't go into a hole in the soil, it went through a hole into a half steel barrel. Every day some guy had to proceed to the site, pull the half-barrel, and dispose of the waste.

Kerosene was poured into the waste and ignited. It was constantly mixed and more kerosene added as needed until all the waste was burned. I never got stuck on this duty, but men that had the pleasure often stunk for days on end. This task was called sh*t duty. ARVNs manned about half of the firebase through digging holes in the ground and placing shacks over it with one small 8-inch round hole to drop their waste through. They were a civilized people that didn't believe in burning waste. The privies were usually positioned near the wire so we always kept a claymore mine buried behind them. If the firebase was hit, it would have been a perfect place for a dink to hide behind. We had a colorful expression that described what would happen if the privy were to be blown up. Out in the jungle, we dug little cat holes and covered up our waste in order to leave no trace of having been there. Many of the line companies left their trash and waste all over the ground.

On firebases or in the jungle, military hygiene was quite a daily task to keep up with because keeping clean was nearly impossible. There were no showers on most firebases. When a soldier was in the jungle, it was easy to squat or lay down in a stream and get wet. Getting wet was the next best thing to a shower or bath. On a firebase, the only way to bathe was to take a sponge bath or make a trip down to the river. Several times we got permission to take a dip in the river. The Army was granted a free patrol to the river so several guys would stand guard while the others swam around trying to clean themselves in the nude because no one had bathing suits. Nothing ever happened during these trips and we always went to a different area each time. Doing anything on a pattern was dangerous in Nam.

Author bathing in Nam

Brushing teeth was no great problem, but some guys never did brush. Shaving wasn't too big a deal either. The sundry packs had shaving cream and blades. On firebases, daily shaving was mandatory. Out in the jungle, I shaved once a week or just before going into the rear or firebase. Shaving cream really wasn't necessary as the humid jungle kept your face wet all the time. I became very skilled at so called "dry" shaving. Several black guys I knew would use a product called Magic to remove their stubble. It stank terribly. After several weeks in the jungle some guys looked very rough.

In 1970, a new type of soldier came to Viet Nam. Some of these guys had only a few months left in the Army and they were being sent to Nam. They were coming from Germany where they had got into drugs or had other disciplinary problems and having a bad attitude didn't help them much either. They had it made during wartime and had blown it. No sympathy was given to such kind of guys with only a few months scheduled to be in Nam. It may have been a coincidence, but hard drug use was very uncommon until these men arrived mid to late 1970 in Nam.

It was in 1971 that the real problem hit after most of the combat was over. The problems in the USA and Europe were spilling over into Nam. It shocked me after I was a civilian to find out that guys were coming home hooked on heroin. I never even heard of it there, although in Basic Training months before we had been warned that heroin soaked marijuana was being sold in Nam. Some people asked me about it, but many didn't believe me when I said that I didn't see hard drug use going on there.

Chapter 24

EXPLOSIVE POWER

The old WWII grenades were rated as having a 5-yard killing radius. The grenades issued to us in RVN were a lot more dangerous. Instead of a cast iron canister filled with powdered TNT, these little toys had a solid core with a brittle notched wire wrapped around. There were hundreds of little pieces of metal thrown out when one went off. The M-26 fragmentation grenade, which was pineapple-shaped, had no ridges, but had a larger killing radius of 10 meters. The baseball shaped M-33 had a killing radius of 15 meters. I doubt if anyone was able to throw a real curve ball around a tree.

Grenades came with a safety clip that was usually removed immediately. When it was time to use it, the ring connected to a pin was pulled. I don't believe it was possible to pull the pin with ones teeth like in the movies. The grenade was still safe as long as you held the handle close to the grenade and this made it possible to put the pin back in if necessary. When it was thrown, the handle fell off and you had three seconds before it went off. We were careful not to lose frags because the enemy would have loved to exchange their marginal grenades for ours.

Our ARVN allies at FSB Rifle once discarded some grenades into the FSB dump. When the refuse was being burned, a few went off. One time, we had to check all the lot numbers on our frags as we called them, as a bad batch had been sent to Nam. Some had gone off after one second. A frag dropped in the open was very dangerous. This happened late in my tour in B Company of the O Deuce. Several months later when we got into close combat we were requesting concussion grenades instead of frags. Concussion grenades could be dropped into a bunker with desired results and if they were thrown back they were relatively harmless in the open. The old pineapple grenades were great for just throwing into the jungle behind the wires. It kept the NVA sappers in ulcers and would break up the monotony of night watch.

Grenades also had another use that I observed twice in Nam. One day, we had thoroughly scouted out an area and stopped for a while at a small pond. Apparently someone remembered the spot and said that there were fish in the hole. A couple of well-placed grenades were dropped in. Several muffled explosions were heard and some foggy air came to the surface. A few minutes later some small catfish were floating on the surface of the water. This was not exactly sport fishing and I don't even remember if the fish were even eaten. Six months later we were doing the same thing and the Colonel caught us doing it. It may have contributed to our L.T. being replaced.

Another time we were walked over to the ARVN side of FSB Rifle to look at a claymore mine. An ARVN soldier one morning noticed the claymore he set out the night before had been tampered with. A sapper, as we called them, had sneaked up at night and taken the ARVN's claymore and replaced it with one packed full of mud instead of C-4. It was a very clear message to all of us that they were out there even if they were not active. Claymores had to be inspected every day and it was best to move them to different locations every night. One of our guys commented that the sapper might have just wanted the C4 from the claymore to cook his rice.

One time, a former North Vietnamese officer gave a sapper demonstration for us. He stripped down to his boxers and slowly started to work his way through the wire. He had little clips that he would use to hold the wires apart. Soon he had finished a little tunnel through the wire. All this was done while he carried a folding stock AK-50 and a string of satchel charges. There was a question and answer session. One grunt asked where they would come through the wire and then pointed out two likely spots. One had a slight ravine going through the wire and also a privy for visual protection for sappers. The other area was the spot where patrols entered in and out of the wire perimeter at one end of Recons spot on the perimeter. Nothing was done to improve either's defenses.

Chapter 25

DISASTER

On Feb 10th 1970, the brass came down to the Recon Platoon and gave us what seemed to be a little mission. Army Intelligence discovered that some NVA might be using abandoned FSB Brick about a click and a half farther west as a base camp. A heavy squad of Recon led by Platoon Sgt. Kelly Torres was to travel there and check it out. I was selected to go along and remember thinking "aw shucks," back into the dangerous jungle again. I would've been much better off being left on the safe FSB rifle with a dry cot in a protected bunker. Rifle had never been hit and the whole area had been quiet for weeks. We slipped into the jungle, slowly went over to Brick, and looked around. Nothing was happening other than the jungle trying to reclaim bare land.

We set up in an area that had a view of FSB Rifle in the distance. Early in the morning, we heard several explosions over on FSB Rifle. At first we thought that they were being mortared. Soon there were green Communist bloc tracers going into Rifle and red American tracers going out. It was a colorful sight, but we were all worried about our fellow Recon guys. FSB Rifle was being hit and we watched the explosions and rifle fire for about

82

ten minutes. Then artillery from other FSBs started dropping flares and high explosive rounds. The HE rounds were popping around the perimeter. Some of the explosions were probably outgoing mortar rounds. Flares were kept going all night until dawn. We knew that the side of FSB Rifle that had been hit was where the rest of our Platoon was located.

When we finally got in contact by radio, we were told to be vigilant and come back in the morning, but none of us could sleep that night. The walk back in the next morning was done very slowly because the enemy could have been on our path. Our worst fears were realized. Before we even got back through the wire, we were told that three from Recon had died and multiple men had been wounded. Ray Moon, Marlin Peterson, and Harold Shuler were the three. Two other Echo company guys also were killed and several other Americans. Marlin was one of the three guys that I had come out to FSB Rifle with. Harold was a family man that frequently read the Bible. Ray was a very likable guy from Salt Lake. Eight guys had died in just a few minutes. Many more were wounded. Most never came back and about half of Recon was gone.

Ray Moon

I was told this is what happened. The sappers had hit the piled up sandbags in front of two of the bunkers with RPGs or rocket-powered grenades. The sapper team had entered through the slit in the wire where patrols entered and exited. A dozen sappers immediately ran into an opening and ran down the row of bunkers throwing satchel charges and shooting into the bunkers where some guys were still in their cots sleeping. Satchel charges were one-pound blocks of explosives with a primitive pull string type fuse and detonator. They were similar to our concussion grenades only a lot more crude. In a closed bunker or foxhole the blast would kill a man. Everything was going their way until they got down to the last few bunkers that Recon was manning.

At least one NVA sapper went to them a satchel charge into the command post of the FSB. CSM Walter Sabalauski had positioned himself prone on the ground with his M16. The command post was saved.

One Recon guy went into his bunker to get his combat web belt and a sapper shot into the bunker, but fortunately the sapper missed. One of Recon's senior Sergeants had time to escape out of his bunker and positioned himself a little higher up on the hill. Soon a sapper was almost upon him and behind the roof of a bunker. The sapper then shot a burst out of his folding stock AK-50 at the Sergeant. The Sergeant ducked behind his cover and avoided death by mere inches. He then shot a burst back at the sapper, but missed. This went on three or four times until the Sergeant got real savvy and waited with his Mike16 pointed at the spot where the sapper last showed himself. When the enemy stuck his head back out, the Sergeant blew his head clean off.

This all occurred close to where my bunker was located and around the same time, the few remaining Recondos and other troops started to rally. Panic set in among the sappers when their lead man was decapitated. The area where the sappers came through the wire was now blocked. NVA were great at making elaborate battle plans and initiated them very well, but fortunately for Americans, they had a tendency to get confused when something went wrong. Self-initiative was never evident among Communists. The remaining sappers had not planned on how to get away if the slit in the wire was blocked. I was told they went down by the wire and were trying to get through when a patient grunt pulled the clacker on a claymore mine buried under some napalm barrels. The remaining sappers were all killed.

The morning after was spent rebuilding the bunkers. Filling sandbags with soil that contained blood and little bits of flesh wasn't fun. We put all the mess back into the bags. Papers, pens, bits of uniform all went into the bags. After that, I had a great respect for the penetrating ability of rocket-powered grenades or RPGs. In the future whenever I built a bunker or moved into an old one, I always put an extra row of sandbags in front. Two rows were not sufficient. The bunker that I had been using had not been blown, but there were parts of human brain nearby. I had to cover it up because it bothered me to see it. I was still green and not used to seeing human remains, but this too would eventually pass. I would see a lot more fresh brains in the next few months.

The bodies of all the Americans and NVA had been flown out before we got back from Brick. Dane McNabb and Kelly Torres, the two most senior guys in Recon, went to the morgue and identified the guys from Recon and Echo Company. Both guys had been in Nam three years and they both left within a month of the incident.

Dane McNabb, lower left

Months later body identification would become my duty. I had a little talk with Ron "Sid" Meese who had been with me in NCO school and at Ft. Carson. He was on Rifle the night of the attack and showed me a letter he had written. He never mailed it because it stated how boring Nam was. Nothing ever happened, etc. Ron carried that letter with him until he went home from Nam.

It was a daily reminder to stay vigilant, never get lazy or let your guard down, and most importantly never complain about boredom. The history of the 2/502 in Vietnam is very mum about what happened on FSB Rifle. I often wonder who gave Army Intelligence the tip about NVA on FSB Brick. Was it the same girls in Hue? How did the NVA know that Recon would be gone that night and the lines would be thin? When I now ask guys for more detail, or for help checking on the accuracy of my memory on what happened that morning I get no answer. The pain of the memories is too great for them.

A few days after things had settled down, Recon held a small service for its three fallen troopers. Three M16s with bayonets attached were driven into the yellow soil of FSB Rifle. Boonie hats were then placed on the butt ends of the rifles and Jungle boots were placed on the ground. A few words were spoken in memory of the men that were killed and those in the hospital. It was a very subdued gathering and I was still ill at ease even though I knew of this type of service from the movies. Most guys were like me and still in a state of shock. I regret that months later we didn't do the same when other guys were lost. We soon had multiple new replacements for our dead and many wounded that never returned to our unit.

Replacements Ron Sippel, Gary Walker,
Glenn Fischer, Tom Boyce, among others

Chapter 26

RADIOHEAD

Shortly before the tragedy on FSB Rifle, I was asked to be the CP radio and telephone operator or RTO for Recon. I never saw a state side-like telephone while in RVN. The job had many duties. Recon consisted of three squads when at full strength. Each squad usually had an RTO, as did the platoon command post, which consisted of the platoon leader, platoon Sergeant, and two RTOs. The squad RTOs and the other RTO in the CP carried a PRC-25. It was commonly called a prick 25 because it weighed about twenty-five to thirty pounds.

I got the honor of carrying an even slightly heavier encrypted version. Included with it was a code wheel that had a different code for each day of the month. Every month a new one would be issued. Every day I had to change the code settings. I was amazed. It never failed in the months that I carried it. The code radio was used for communicating with BN on sensitive issues. Externally all talk was encoded. The NVA could listen in and did as we found out later. When talking in the open it was necessary to use as much slang, idioms, and nonsense synonyms as possible. I was very impressed by L.T. Ciccolella's ability to speak in a fashion that an NVA well versed in British English would have a difficult time understanding. The most important thing to do was never say anything over the open air that the enemy could use such as names, position, unit, size of unit, etc.

We all had numbers assigned to us called packs. The platoon leader kept this with him. If a guy had a bad case of jungle rot on his feet, I would say that pack number 12's dogs have the crud and he needs to come in for refreshment. If the PL was going to meet up with another unit, he would say that we would dance over and fuse with you. After a few weeks, a person became very good at this nonsense talk that had real meaning. Other companies also had encoder radios. If something important needed to be discussed with one of the other companies we both would switch over to the coded radio.

I once had a PRC-5 go bad when out on a daylong ambush in a squad size unit. It was a situation that would have been very dangerous if we made contact with the enemy. They sent a chopper out to get us and the radio was strong enough to communicate when they got within a 100 meters. Disposing of batteries on re-supply day was a ritual. After the new battery was put in the radio, the wires to all cells in the old battery were bared and wrapped together. A small hole was then dug in the soil and the battery covered. The cells would get very hot and begin to pop. We didn't want to leave a usable battery for the NVA to use on booby traps. One time when we passed through an area where I had buried a battery I noticed that it had been dug out of the ground.

Supply day was always a lot of work and worry for me. As head RTO, I had to very carefully order all the supplies needed for at least three days. This included food, clothing, munitions, and a host of other things. I did mess up a few times. One time extra ammo came in. We kept it and a few days later it was needed badly. A lot of guys actually liked having an extra bandolier of 5.56 ammo strung across their body. It made them look like Poncho Villa.

In late February the monsoons were gone but it still rained frequently. We went on a mission to an area on the coastal plain. It was dry enough to send trucks off to Rifle to pick us up. I walked down to the trucks with the guys. Just as we were loading up, I noticed that the encryption wheel was missing from my pocket. I ran the hundred yards back up the hill and found it lying where I had just cooked a meal. The fatigue bottom pocket was unbuttoned and it had fallen out. I ran back down the hill and caught my truck with seconds to spare. A month earlier an officer had lost one and he never got promoted on schedule. I probably would have been busted down to private and had shit duty forever. It was serious business. No room for error.

One advantage of having a radio was that you could listen to music over the hand set. I never did this in the field, but occasionally did in the rear or when some other guy was doing the work. In the field, no civilian radios were allowed. On firebases, they were tolerated if you weren't on the bunker line. Unfortunately, I showed a guy with no common sense this way of keeping up on the tunes. He immediately started talking over the music and interrupted the volunteer DJ. The DJ got mad and told him to bug off, but it did no good. This guy later became an RTO after I left the field.

By tying up the radio for an entire night, he may have cost some guys getting wounded during a mortar attack. This guy was messing around with the radio when the sound of a mortar tube could be heard. He refused to give it up so the general location of the tube could be called in. When he was finally threatened and gave the radio up, it was too late.

In the rear, anything went with music. In Recon we had two guys with cassette players. Unfortunately, they had only about six tapes between them. Four of the six were country; the other two were the best of Neil Diamond and a Jackson Five album. I can remember Charlie Pride singing, "The snakes crawl at night" at least a thousand times. The same could be said of Chet Atkins strumming. Many years later Charlie Pride visited Helena Montana when I lived there. I stopped by the hardware store where Charlie was doing a promotion and told him the story. Later in my tour in Nam, many of the REMFs bought into an eight track-buying club. It was always interesting to come back from a mission and hear a new song and try and guess who was singing it.

Chapter 27

THE UGLINESS OF SOME

It was a nice day and the sun was shining. It was interesting watching the countryside change from jungle and then to tropical grass covered foothills. We were being trucked from the jungle to an area in the flat rice growing areas. Trouble soon started. Somebody threw a smoke grenade a few trucks ahead of us for some reason. One of our guys had obtained a few tear gas grenades a few weeks before and the sight of the smoke grenade got his mischievous brain going. We soon came to a guard shack next to a bridge. As we were driving by he threw a tear gas grenade into the shack manned by two ARVNs. This would have been cute except they came out and leveled their M16s at the back of our truck. Luckily they didn't shoot into us. His peers reprimanded the guy and this got him more upset.

In about 5 miles we were in a densely populated area. There was a Catholic school or orphanage with a courtyard full of children. Two or three Nuns were with the children. Without any warning the guy tossed his last tear gas grenade over the wall into the courtyard. The wind was in the right direction to send the gas toward the children. All we could see was little Vietnamese Nuns trying to herd the children away from the gas.

90

It was not a pretty sight. The rest of us immediately reprimanded the guy again. He replied, "What's the big deal? They're only Catholic." Needless to say he found out that there were some Catholics in Recon. The only thing that saved him from getting his rear kicked was L.T. Ciccolella stopping the truck and threatening him with jail time if any more gas was thrown. Most of us were not very proud to be Americans that day.

A little farther down the road the trucks were driving by some children. One Vietnamese kid ran up to the Chaplain who was riding with his hand out the window and stripped the wristwatch off the chaplain's hand. The trucks stopped but the little thief had melted into the village. The Chaplain was furious and spoke some words that I'm sure he regretted later. We all understood his frustration. Another lesson was learned about watching out for little children.

Vietnamese pedestrians and vehicle drivers had a New York City attitude. They would not get out of the way if they knew you saw them. Many Army drivers learned to just rev their engines and go. If you tooted your horn they would just ignore you because they knew you saw them. On an earlier trip I saw a Vietnamese man hit and killed by a truck playing this game. There were no traffic cops or rules in the whole country.

Chapter 28

CONFLICTS

Andy was a good guy to know, but when he had a few beers in him he liked to get in fights. We were all back at Camp Eagle and Andy and a few others got into a fight with some guys from another Recon unit up at the Brigade enlisted man's club called the Phoc Roc. They came back and wanted to get reinforcements, but nobody was in a mood to fight so it appeared that was to be the end of it.

Andy getting pen tattoo by Tri

Later that evening I went up the hill to the Phoc Roc to find someone. He wasn't there so I started down the hill. Guys were standing all over the hillside talking and drinking. On the way down to the company area, someone asked me if I'm from Recon O'Deuce. Being a dumb farm boy, I said, "Yeah." The guy sucker punched me and soon four black guys were kicking me on the ground. I managed to get up, get one good in the nose and run down the hill to friendly confines. If they had been sober, I probably would have been killed or at least hospitalized.

Andy and I were both the same height and similar looking. In addition, only Recon units wore woodland camouflage. I don't believe it was a racial incident, but it developed into one. Word soon got around that some cowards had jumped "Brink" and we were going to get them. In retrospect, I should never have mentioned how my face got messed up. The next night the whole Recon Platoon went over to pay a visit to the culprits. They had all gone back to the field except for a malingerer. The poor guy was harassed for about five minutes and we left the area after trashing it. Unfortunately, someone slashed the tents in the company area.

The next night of the stand down started out very mellow. Just about the whole Recon Platoon and the rest of CO E were standing around sipping beer in the hot evening. All of a sudden about twenty blacks approached. About five of them had M16s. Soon we were accused of being racist, and they even threatened us. No one in Recon was armed at the time. Three different guys tried to talk to their leader. It was soon obvious that one guy from Recon had a plan to defuse the situation. He just kept talking to the guy for what seemed an eternity arguing each point in a low key and dignified manner. Recon like all Army units was multiracial. At that time only one black was in our unit, but it was far from being lily white.

After about half an hour, the accusation was made that the "N" word had been used the night before. I had not heard it said, but it might have been. One of the old timers said, "Hey if it was said we're sorry – now you better be leaving." Nobody had left or seemed the slightest bit intimidated by the whole scene. If the

M16s were going to be used they would have been fired right away. They stayed in the area for a while longer arguing every point that could be made. By then most of us had realized nothing was going to happen. About that time L.T. Ciccolella showed up and told the ringleader to leave or he would soon be in trouble. I can't remember if the famous LBJ or Long Binh Jail was brought up in the threat.

What had started out as a long-standing feud between two units had changed into a racial, incident and I had been in the middle of it. In my nine months in the field, I never saw any racial ill feelings between guys in Recon. The ringleader and I would meet again.

During the next stand down, I got into several incidents. The first incident involved a basic lack of knowledge of flags. One night, I walked into my hooch and my friend Vega from Mortar Platoon was there along with several other Puerto Ricans. They had a flag up on the wall that I thought was the Cuban flag. Without even thinking twice, I asked where they obtained the Cuban flag. There was nothing but dead silence and Doberman-like cold stares from all of them. Finally Vega said very sternly that it was the Puerto Rican flag, *not* the Cuban flag and then explained that they look similar. I said that I was sorry about the mistake and walked on. I have never since confused the two flags. After that, for penance the outside of my room became the Latino hangout in the company area and it worked out well. No one kicked my door in or stole my poncho liner again. I had learned over a year before that once you are friends with Hispanics they will stick up for you.

During the summer, racial relations improved slightly in the O Deuce. In the field, they were very good. In the rear there was de facto segregation with little animosity. None of the white guys seemed to care that a lot of black guys carried canes with the black power clenched fist on the top. One night, I was busy tending bar when I looked up and saw this guy all dressed up in camouflage with a black beret that had the words *Black Revolutionary* embroidered across the front. We stared at each other for a few seconds, and I realized we had met before. He had once held a 16 on Recon. I looked at him and asked what was going to happen to me when he won the revolution? I then handed him a free beer. Not much was said, but we had made peace and said hello to each other a few times later.

One time one of our more jovial guys was bantering with our Kit Carson scout, Tri. He called Tri a gook in a joking manor. Tri went ballistic and yelled, "Me no gook, me no gook" and started threatening our lives and body parts. The cultural line had been crossed. Vietnamese are very serious people that you have to be on very good terms with and know them well before joking. The Recondo thought he was close enough that he could joke a little.

We always called the North Vietnamese Army soldiers gooks (pronounced in the Strike Force as guks). This term was almost never used for the people and soldiers of the ARVN. They were very sensitive people, and it was their country. I got a little amused one time when a directive came down from Division that the term "The Little People" was never to be used in our nonsense talk over the radio when referring to ARVN soldiers. Apparently one of the ARVN upper officers got upset when he found out the term was being used to describe his Army. Munchkins, Lilliputians, or elves probably would have slipped by his censorship. In the '70s, the same thing happened in the USA when "Short People" hit the pop music charts.

Chapter 29

NEW LEADERS – NEW CHALLENGES

One day, a new 1st L.T. came to Recon and said that he was going to be our Platoon Leader. L.T. Ciccolella went on to a new position and later after Captain Asher's death became Captain of E Company. His name was James Thomas Hill and he was another Airborne Ranger. He came to introduce himself to his command post and immediately looked me over. He then told me that a Sgt. Brinker at Jump School had singled him out for special treatment. That is, lots of extra pushups. He did this with a half serious scowl on his face. I had heard this a few times before how this all Army tough black Sergeant loved to dote his time on young white officers in a school where rank meant nothing. He then laughed a little and I knew that my family name had brought back to him memories of the recent past.

In early March, the whole 2/502 went south to an area just north of Da Nang. The mountains went right down to the ocean. There was a very high, but flat-topped mountain called Bach Ma where Teddy Roosevelt once went tiger hunting. The French had a summer villa on top that was now in ruins. Some of the old timers remembered patrolling around it in 1969. We were just north of the mountain and had a nice view of the magnificent waterfall. Tri our Kit Carson scout did a funny thing on the side of the mountain. It was very hot and after a very hard walk, he held his nose and jumped into the bottom of a pool. It was kind of nice seeing him lying in 6 feet of crystal clear water, cooling off.

Tri cooling off

One afternoon we were in a large grassy meadow area north of the mountain and decided to start a baseball game while waiting for orders. It was mid afternoon and sunny. We found an old stick and used something as a ball. All of a sudden, a group of Vietnamese civilians started walking toward us. They were merchants selling all kinds of wares. Warm beer and soda were sold along with little loaves of white flour bread.

Playing ball at Bach Ma, "Okie" batting
Photo compliments of Dave Hepburn

L.T. Hill, still being new to Recon, wasn't too happy that we were buying the bread. The traveling merchants wanted $1.00 for the sodas and beer, but unfortunately for them, we refused to pay that much. The soda and beer were safe because they were canned. We all bought the little loaves in the pastoral meadow. The situation appeared like a majestic scene right out of Eden next to the mountain and the waterfalls.

The bread tasted very good to guys that were used to eating Charlie Rats and LRRPs. Soon their local leader was trying to sell one of the girls. One of our medics said that he would check her out to see if she was clean. Being a biologist, I was rolling my head in disbelief. Microbiologists are still trying to find a rapid diagnostic test for sexually transmitted diseases. The L.T. put a stop to any potential deals and all the Vietnamese left in disgust.

We made it look like we were going to camp there. As soon as it was dark we slithered over to the mountain and slipped into the jungle. It was uncomfortable sleeping on the hillside, but that was better that getting killed if we stayed in the field. The group had probably counted every man and weapon in our group. Mortars RPGs and AKs probably would have worked the area over that night.

I should have known that it was a bad omen the day a second medic was sent out to Recon. He came at a time when Recon was doing a lot of hard humping (hiking) up mountains. He was terribly out of shape because he spent six months down by Saigon working in a VD clinic putting silver needles in little brown butts. To make matters worse he fell down and ripped the bottom of his fatigues open. The sight of a pink butt surrounded by jungle camo walking ahead of you was down right hilarious. He soon was one of us and became a close friend. Dennis Moreau was one of the bravest men that I ever met in Nam.

Chapter 30

DEATH COMMAND

One of our guys had volunteered for sniper school about one month before. While we were at Bach Ma he rejoined us. He was now toting an XM-21 experimental sniper rifle. It was a finely tuned custom M-14 with a special barrel. He had two telescopes for it. The daylight scope had reticule demarcations out over 1000 meters. There was also a starlight scope for use at night that amplified light and gave an image in black and green. I got to try a Starlite scope stateside and could hit human sized targets at 350 meters in the dark using an M16. We were all waiting to see what it could do. Opportunity unfortunately came too soon.

We were flown to a nearby hill and linked up with a line company. It was a very clear day and we could see the beautiful north side of Bach Ma. In a meadow between the mountain and us, a group of twenty people were soon seen milling around. Most of us thought they were woodcutters. VC would not run around in the daylight within sight of a hill covered with GIs. The guy with the scope wanted to nail one of them. An officer with us said no because they looked like woodcutters. A higher officer said he would check with the Vietnamese to see if anyone was supposed to be there. A few minutes later word came back that no friendlies were in the area. The officer protested vehemently and was relieved of his command.

The sniper got all ready and the line-company with us was loaded on choppers. When all was ready the sniper took aim. The distance was at the limit of the rifle, but no wind was blowing. At the appointed time, he fired a single round and I saw a man throw up his hands and fall. A minute later the choppers came in on an air assault. Two more were killed before the guys from the company stopped firing. There wasn't any shooting back. Woodcutters can only throw axes. I still have admiration for the dismissed officer because he had stood his moral ground. If he had been at Mai Lai two years earlier things would have been different. No one talked about this incident because some RVN political man and an over eager upper American officer had killed three innocent people.

The image of a sniper is someone who kills a lot and is in very little danger, yet this was far from reality. Snipers went out in teams of two to do their work. If you were inept or unlucky, the enemy might spy you first. This happened once in our BN. We were just getting ready to call it a day. Even some bedrolls were already out. I got a call from BN TOC and gave the horn to L.T. Hill. A pair of snipers realized at sunset that they had been spotted and were surrounded. They could hear the encircling movements and the enemy had shown himself hoping to draw fire. The outcome didn't look very good for the two guys that night. We were being asked to get ready to chopper over and save them. The whole plan didn't look good to us. Flying in at sunset was not good odds. As it turned out, they managed to get the team out without our help.

Chapter 31

FATAL ERRORS

While we were at the Bach Ma area, another tragedy happened. Line companies frequently set up NDTs (Night Defensive Targets) around their night position. The forward observer would call in artillery at a safe distant target and bring it in as close as safety would allow. If needed that night no time would be wasted in adjusting fire. The first round out would be right where it was first needed. We were working as a Battalion, and the four line companies and Recon each had a different night position.

A FO (Forward Observer) from one of the companies was setting up his NDTs when the first shell out hit another line company's position. I think two guys were killed by so-called friendly fire. One guy only had a day left in Nam. Grunt fatalism said that if you were going to buy the farm it should happen when you first get to Nam not after you suffered in Nam for a full year. We were all demoralized. Someone had called in the map coordinates of his unit wrong. I don't know which unit it was. Death was always around when grunts started playing with lethal toys. A soldier has to be 100% all the time or face death.

During the next month, Recon worked by itself in a large AO south of Hue under the leadership of L.T. Hill and we saw a lot of combat. We were very successful, but sometimes things went wrong. One time we set up in an area and a heavy patrol went out to check the surroundings. The point man was very alert and snuck up on a small NVA camp. The men fired at the camp, but didn't get all of them. There was a blood trail leading up a hill and they went on line and went up the hill after them. There was an exchange of gunfire and two NVA were finished off. My look-alike Andy had his thumb shot off. I was told that he yelled out, "Look, I'm going home." When the patrol came back they brought everything of value.

The remaining surviving gooks had no shelter or supper that night and had to explain to their leaders how they had messed up. The medivac took Andy to the hospital. He was in terrible pain and had lost his bravado. I saw many wounded guys in Nam. The only two that ever cried out in pain had finger wounds. One interesting thing that was brought back from the NVA camp was a medical book. It was hand copied with colored pencils. I had studied to be a biologist and realized that hands were perfect.

Another find was a written letter ready to be sent to the wife of one of the BN officers. The NVA had probably found a letter of his and was using his return address to send a nonsense letter. To us, it looked amateurish and comical. It would have probably been very unsettling to the officer's wife. All of the stuff from the site was sent back for Army intelligence to sort out. The NVA must have had a psychological operations branch just like we did.

There were a lot of enemies in the area but they were somewhat stupid. We sometimes rivaled with them for that title. We had a new guy on OP one noon hour. He saw this dink walking down the trail toward him. He let go a full magazine out of his 16 and sprayed the treetops. L.T. Hill sat him down and gave him a fatherly lecture on keeping your cool. He said, "Take your rifle off safety, aim, and shoot in small bursts until the job is done. Remember he is carrying his AK over his shoulder and you have the element of surprise. Take your time and get him because that night he may come after you." This scene is somewhat similar to the one out of *Platoon* where Charlie Sheen freezes.

A couple of days later, almost the same scene happened at noon. This time the OP hit the gook and he ran away leaving a blood trail. His AK, which he later dropped, probably kept him from getting killed immediately because it took several rounds that would have hit the dink in the upper chest. BN said that they wanted to send out a tracker team. They arrived shortly, and two expert trackers and their dog started following the trail. A couple of hundred yards down the hill the blood trail led into a hole in the thickest underbrush. No one wanted to go in. He was listed as dead and he probably did die of his wounds.

By this time, I started to believe the NVA were the opposite of deer. They liked to move at noon rather than early morning or late afternoon. When they were wounded, however, they liked to run downhill and into the brush just like deer.

Chapter 32

THE KILLING CONTINUES

We soon returned to the FSB Rifle area. This time Recon had the all of AO as the line companies went elsewhere. We were moved to a new area every few days. Frequently more than one LZ was prepped with artillery and sometimes the choppers did false insertions. The NVA thought that the area was theirs; it was theirs to die in. We kept catching them off guard and then the body count started.

Another time a squad found a small camp of NVA. They all got away, but lost everything except the shirts on their backs. A lot of praise was given to a fellow Iowan's savvy in combat. L.T. Hill managed to find a pistol in one of the gook hooches. We were all jealous of him. He wisely kept it rather than giving it to a chopper pilot with instructions to take it to the O Deuce area.

One time we had another kill and I dragged the body into a shell crater to bury it. I always did this whenever possible, yet others gave me grief about what I thought was a good deed. I thought it was the decent thing to do, and I was keeping the Recon tradition of leaving no trace behind.

We then went off on another combat assault. Before we came in, several LZs were prepped with artillery again. This served several purposes such as confusing the enemy as to where we were assaulting and also giving us the means to destroy any anti-helicopter Chinese claymore mines that might be set up.

As we were going in, some gook was shooting back at us. The L.T. called hot LZ, threw a red smoke grenade, and we disembarked under fire. The rest of the Platoon got in without any problem and the LZ was secured.

We moved out, but there was no more firing. We found one dead dink all torn up by artillery and chunks of metal were stuck in him. Then we found a severed leg and a blood trail leading into some more thick brush. There are times when even hardcore Veterans balk at doing something. Nobody would go in the hole after the one-footed foe. Finally L.T. Hill went in with his pistol and pulled him out. The enemy soldier had taken dynamite cord and used it as a tourniquet to stop the bleeding from his leg. His leg had been cut off as flat as a shank of ham in a butcher's shop.

We all admired this enemy soldier's bravado. He had the ability to tie up his leg in a macho way and still shoot at us. When I reported the results over the radio to the firebase the arty guys could be heard cheering over the radio. They needed a little positive reinforcement now and again.

A few days later, the line companies returned to the now active AO. One day I was listening on the radio and one of them called BN in a very excited manner and said how they had found something smelly at an LZ. When the coordinates were called in, I realized that they had found my buried body from the week before. I got on the radio and advised the company to let Recon's gook rest in peace. We were all getting cocky and too hardcore.

One time we were on a firebase and a commotion broke out. Some observant guy on the base had looked out on the mostly open area to the east and saw a lone figure walking about a click out. Soon it was decided to let a guy with an M-60 machine gun use tracers and try to get him. A crowd gathered and cheered the gunner as he tried to get the solitary enemy. The guy ran all over the place looking for a spot to get away. Soon it was like a Celtics-Lakers game in the '80s with a large group cheering on the gunner. The lone enemy soldier finally got into some brush and disappeared. It was not a very pretty scene, but it broke the boredom of FSB duty one sunny day. If the guy down range survived the war, he is probably still telling his story in some Vietnamese Veteran's Club.

Chapter 33

DUST, DINING, AND DUSTY MINES

When we went on a combat assault, our M16s were locked and loaded, but left on safe. Some units made the troopers keep an empty chamber until combat was imminent. We would hold them vertically inside the chopper. Seat belts were not used and sometimes when a Huey or Slick, as we frequently called them, banked hard on a turn you could see straight down at Mother Earth. Only centrifugal force kept you from falling out. After a while you got used to flying this way. Many new guys white knuckled it on their first rides.

View coming in on combat assault

The M16s had what we called a cherry cap over the muzzle to keep out dirt. It was black plastic about the size and shape of a shot shell. The Army started to pass them out because so many guys were buying unsightly condoms to protect the muzzles of their rifles. The first bullet out would blow the cap away without any problem. We usually wrapped our rifles with the ever-present green towel that every grunt had. This would keep out most dust and could be removed rapidly. This was very necessary during the dry summer season when LZs were extremely dusty. The rotors of the choppers would make a dust storm that would cover a sweaty body and fill an M16 with dirt. For a while we were given some experimental zip-lock plastic bags for our M16s, but they were too slow to remove on air assaults. The towel worked best.

After the usual flying around and artillery preps the hueys would come down to an almost hover about 3 feet off the ground. Jumping off was the only way down from the skids. This was not always fun with a heavy backpack. I went several months with a sore hip from jumping off choppers with a hundred pound load on my back. The guys would run to the perimeter of the LZ and protect it until all choppers were unloaded. That was the end of airmobile and the beginning of leg.

One night while back in the Rifle AO, we moved into a site that we had used months before. A man named "Hutch" Hutchinson even picked out the same sleeping spot that he had used previously. While he was clearing the spot to lay his bedroll, he heard a clink at the end of his knife. The spot was carefully inspected revealing a detonator for a land mine that was just even with the surface. The mine was removed from the soil. It was not a mine in the traditional sense, but a 60mm mortar round with a mine's detonator on top. It had obviously been in the ground a long time because it was corroded. Hutch was upset because he realized that a few months before he had slept on a land mine. If he had walked on the area before, it might have gone off. Laying on it had spread his weight around. I never saw us use an old site to set up again. Life could so easily be lost even while sleeping.

The same evening that we found Hutch's mine, L.T. Hill talked us into making boonie rat stew. Everyone contributed one can of something, and then red sauce was liberally used to douse it. It was heated up in an old ammo can. All of this was a lot of fun except the stew was terrible. L.T. Hill's feelings were hurt that we didn't like it. In his later rise to General he was probably never in charge of a menu or his career would have been cut short. We never tried communal cooking again, but no one died from the stew either. We blamed Alpha Company for not teaching him how to cook when he was a cherry.

One time L.T. Hill decided to re-teach us basic patrolling. The point man found some old bunkers and hooches within a short distance. Some of the old timers said Recon had killed a dink there in '69, yet the trouble was that I had heard the story before and it kept changing. So far three guys had stated or implied that they got the kill. The hero who supposedly killed this dink had tried to make my life miserable just a few months before. This guy had fashioned himself a hero because he and the two other guys had opened up on a lone enemy soldier. I just shook my head. L.T. Hill had us blow the bunkers so they couldn't be used again. The skeletal remains were still there and a fresh Widowmaker card was attached along with a Chu Hoi leaflet. These were leaflets scattered all over the jungle telling the enemy how to give themselves up, but why would the enemy give up. We were killing their brethren any chance we received.

Chapter 34

FUN IN THE SUN
WITH SOME R & R

One day Col. Young made the mistake of asking Recon if there was anything we needed. And boy oh boy did he get an earful. A loud cry went up to send us to Eagle Beach. Eagle Beach was a nice strip of fine yellow sand on the South China Sea east of Hue. It was a fenced in area surrounded by villages. We got to see a lot of Oriental buildings and even some rice paddies on the way. I am proud to say that I never walked in a rice paddy. Some fishermen were in the process of making nuoc mam, their smelly fish powder. I even saw a troop of Vietnamese Boy Scouts on a hike.

Once the truck stopped for a few moments in a village, and some guys bought bottles of Vietnamese whiskey. A very pretty half-French girl in a skirt tried soliciting some business while the whiskey was being bartered. The resort consisted of small cottages right next to the beach.

During the day you could go out to the villages and buy souvenirs. I bought a traditional Vietnamese dress and sent it to my sister. At the clubhouse beer was available. One of the favorites was Biere LaRue more commonly known as Tiger Beer. The French had brought in German biermeisters decades before. It was a European style beer with a good kick. A couple of the more adventurous guys went out and found a girl. When the medics heard about this, they administered five million units of penicillin VK into each culprit's rear.

The second night several of us in a highly intoxicated condition went back to the beach. The tide was out and we waded a few hundred yards out into the ocean. Soon the tide started coming back in. We managed to get back by walking in the opposite direction of the large ship out in the ocean. I remember waking up face down on the sand in the morning. Contrary to what was seen at the end of the movie *The Green Berets*, the sun rises from the South China Sea and doesn't set there. It was my only good bash the year I was in Nam.

One funny thing did happen. I forgot to keep my leather civilian wallet dry. It shrank up the next day to about a third of its normal size. My brain and my wallet were in the same condition. I ran into an Iowan that I knew in Basic Training, and he had what we call a REMF job. He came to the beach one day a week on his day off. It was good to see him. Grunts in Nam had it bad compared to the rear echelon types. To some of them it was almost like a vacation in the tropics. Soon it was over and we went back to the field. The best thing that happened was taking several group photos. They were the last photos taken of some of the guys.

Gary Gear, William Kilby, Underhill, Doc Moreau,
Malphrus, Okie, Hutch, Ackerman, William "Alabama" Allred
Gary was KIA shortly after this photo

111

Chapter 35

OPEN LAND AND MONTAGNARDS

One day Col. Young or "Cajun Tiger" addressed us and said the ARVNs would start taking over most of the difficult roles in the defense of the area. The American role would be diminishing. Some wondered if we were going home soon. There was some truth to this because we had a few guys transfer in from the Big Red One Division when it left. They were fine veteran grunts and fit right in except they always said that the Big Red One was a better unit. Soon we left the area south of Hue for a little excursion to a village called Mai Loc, north of Hue. It was a different area than the jungle. Even the open grazing lands of Nam could be dangerous. Nothing of great consequence happened in the area, other than one guy dropping his M16 out of a helicopter.

We detonated a 500-pound bomb that must have failed to explode because it was just lying up on the hillside, and we had to move that night to avoid a brush fire. We were probably in reserve to help the 3rd Brigade, which was running into some tough NVA regulars near FSB Ripcord. We then went to Highway 549, which went west of Hue past the Old Imperial Summer Palace and through the mountains toward the A Shau valley. The Imperial Palace had not been occupied since the 1930s and it was run-down.

Some grunts had machine-gunned the outer wall, which had an enclosed lily pad pond inside the walls. It was not really a highway. It was just a two lane natural dirt road. The Army had used it the two summers before to make excursions into the mystical Valley of Death. Just under a year earlier, in May 1969, the 101st Airborne had fought one of the toughest battles in its history on a mountain called Dong Ap Bia or "Hamburger Hill," as we Americans called it, on the west side of the valley. The valley was a long slit between two rows of mountains. Its direction was almost directly north-south. The NVA had owned it from '65–'68 and used it to prepare for the attack on Hue in Tet of 1968. The weather was always so bad during the monsoons that it was abandoned every fall. We started patrolling the north side of the highway by FSB Bastogne. It was obvious the Division was planning on going back into the valley.

On this trip, we came across a camp of people by the side of the highway. We knew immediately that they were Montagnards. Montagnards were racially different from the Vietnamese and lived in the mountains west of Hue since their ancestors were replaced by the Vietnamese 700 years ago in the coastal rice growing areas along the ocean. This group had been enslaved by the NVA in the A Shau valley. They had recently escaped and the Republic of Viet Nam was resettling them. They had always been abused by whoever was in power. In many places in Nam, they became great friends of Americans, who treated them much better than the Vietnamese. This group had been armed with WWII era weapons. A black soldier asked a Vietnamese woman who these people were, and she told him they were Vietnamese soul brothers. I was a little mystified by this comment.

One time we were patrolling along the road west of Hue. We were near some woodcutters who were salvaging some giant Eucalyptus trees that had been killed by defoliation a few years before. The woodmen were only about two steps ahead of the termites that swarmed in the area every evening. The loggers were kind of fun to watch. Cultural differences exist even in tree

113

cutting. Vietnamese used an ax that was similar to a pickaxe. It had a handle with a pick-like head made of wood at the end. On each end of this wood, a cross member was imbedded with a metal ax head.

It looked silly, but was actually quite ingenious. The shape added balance and the length of the cross member allowed the ax man to cut through giant trees with only a slim notch. A 4 to 5 foot diameter tree could be dropped in a very tidy manor. At the end of the day, L.T. Hill led us down to the trucks and we commandeered a ride about a mile farther west. He didn't trust them. They may have been in communication with the enemy. After the ride west, we slithered again into a nice hiding place and listened to the termites swarm. If the woodcutters had given away our position, it was old news, but our fun in the sun was apparently over.

Chapter 36

STRANGE HAPPENINGS

On one of our first days in the area, a dog team was sent out to help us. We had called in that there was an old bunker complex ahead. The dog and his handler moved out in front of us and the dog gave the alert. The trainer told us that something indeed was out ahead of us. I was then also working as the FO and L.T. Hill decided to drop some arty ahead of us. No 105mm battery was within distance so we were given a 155mm battery. After radioing in our position and direction to target, I asked to have the first shots put out at 400 meters. They replied that unless we were in contact, we had to drop the first rounds at least 600 meters.

The first rounds seemed farther out than 600 meters, but I brought them even closer until we were getting airbursts in the trees ahead of us. After the trees were destroyed, I asked for a few delayed fuse rounds that would explode underground. Everything seemed to be working perfectly, but there was a problem. We went right through the bunker complex and found no gooks. Either the dog had smelled something old or a trail watcher was having his lunch there. When I got back on the horn to report the result of the bombardment, the arty officer asked me if I knew how much money had been spent wiping out some empty bunkers. Arty was now apparently being rationed! How strange that was to hear in war.

A night or two later, I was monitoring the radio when I heard Vietnamese being spoken. Our ARVN allies had their own frequencies to use and shouldn't have been using ours. Sometimes small units would switch to an unused frequency for internal work so it didn't surprise me. The chattering kept on so I rudely said in English that this was a restricted frequency. One of them then asked me who I was in British-style English. I cut the conversation off because giving away anything over the radio was forbidden and unwise. I suspected that the NVA were listening in on the same frequency. We would get this radio back later. Battalion should have heard it also, but nothing was ever said. They probably couldn't hear the weak transmission.

The next day we went down a steep ridge into a narrow valley. When we got to the bottom, I couldn't contact Battalion. It was a scary feeling to be out of contact with help when you needed it. Luckily, when we moved about 50 meters away from the embankment, radio contact was made again. We soon found an extensive old bunker complex that had no signs of recent activity. We dropped some smoke grenades down breathing holes and none came to the surface. At this time, we had a call that some supplies were coming in. The chopper came overhead and started to kick them out since there was no LZ nearby. The first box was a case of light antitank weapons or M-79 LAWs. We found out that the rest of the chopper was loaded with more LAWs.

We told the pilot that we had not ordered these LAWs. He left and we split up the single case of LAWs. They could come in handy. We all wondered what was going on. Was it just another Army snafu? We soon climbed a strange small knob that was ill defined on the map. When we were there we got a message from a chopper above that he wanted us to blow an LZ. The L.T. got on the horn and told him that we would need dynamite, C4, detcord, and blasting caps, etc. in order to complete the job. There was confusion on both sides until we realized it was not one of the Strike Force officers. The chopper then left and we went on our way. Some guys thought that it was a CIA or a Russian chopper. Chances are it was just a lost and embarrassed Colonel from another BN. The whole area gave me the creeps. The BN was opening FSB Veghel at the east side of the A Shau. We had been working just northeast of it in an area that had seen a lot of fighting a few years earlier.

Chapter 37

HILL 714

Recon was assigned to cross a southern tributary of the Song Bo River and to check out a hill that was 714 meters above sea level. On the map it was called Dong A La. It was part of the range that was the eastern edge of the A Shau valley. Two of the three squads were to land on top and go recon the area. I was to stay with the third squad and help in communications. The third squad was ready to go in if help was needed. The choppers inserted the two squads, and they went their separate ways to check out different areas of the hill. In a couple of hours the choppers went back in to pick them up. They had seen nothing at the top of Hill 714.

As the choppers were leaving some NVA started shooting at them. It was a chilling feeling. Why had they shot at choppers that were leaving? The answer was only too clear; they wanted us to come back. These gooks were obviously not afraid of us; they wanted to fight. Within a very short time, Recon returned to 714 and brought along Bravo Company. The next month is still somewhat of a blur to me.

We were told that shortly before another BN from the 1st Brigade had grenades dropped on them from high in the trees in this area and they ran, leaving a lot of equipment behind. It seemed like kind of a tall tale, but the treetops were now being watched. This was primitive jungle that had not been defoliated. Trails and roads under the triple canopy could not be seen easily from the air. We soon found plenty of well-used trails that led in all directions. They were well maintained like those of the Appalachian Trail.

In a very short time the lead element of Bravo Company made contact. Recon was on top of a knob and could see the lead element of Bravo about 10 yards from the red flash of returning fire. We put some fire over the top of the line company. Within a few seconds, some dink down below noticed us up on the hill and let go several long bursts. We could hear the whistling of the rounds going by us. That was the only time in Nam I heard bullets going by. All future combat was so close that the muzzle blast of the AK-47s covered up the whistling of the bullets. The NVA soon took off leaving one of their dead. Bravo Company also had some dead and wounded. It's never easy seeing a guy wrapped up in his poncho ready to be sent home.

My M16 had jammed twice in the firefight, which wasn't good at all. One of the guys from Bravo that had been wounded left his M16 lying on the ground. His war was over at least for a little while. I exchanged bolts with the other rifle and did a few bursts, and it worked perfectly. I used the H & R Mike16 with a stainless steel Colt bolt until June with no more malfunctions. A few weeks earlier, I had etched the name Jeannie on my 16 after my girlfriend in Minnesota who wrote nice pep talk letters.

Chapter 38

RIFLES – BOOBY TRAPS –
MONKEY TALK

Many arguments have been made about which was the better assault rifle, the M16 or the AK-47. The AK was more dependable and had the big 30 round magazine. I know of two guys that AK fire missed because it was too difficult for the enemy soldiers to lay prone with one and fire with the big banana magazine. Taking the magazine out was also difficult. With a 16, all you had to do was push a button and the magazine fell out and at the same time the other hand jammed in another magazine. I always had little leather shoestring loops attached to the bottom of my magazines so they would come out of the ammo pouches more easily.

Some Americans and North Vietnamese also taped two magazines together back to back, but we frowned upon this because dirt and other debris could get into the open magazine. It probably worked better for the enemy, but for us, all we had to do was press the button. You could throw out a lot of lead with a 16. Once we got by the initial burst, we usually had the advantage in a firefight. A single 16, when used properly with short bursts, could sweep a large area in a relatively short period of time. The best thing about the M16 was its bullet. It was a small and fast

5.56mm and could make hamburger out of flesh. The AK-47 round or 7.62x39 would punch a hole in you, but not cause much damage beyond the hole. I once took a look at an NVA soldier's head that had been hit by a 16. The hole going in was smaller than that of a pencil, but the exit wound was 4 inches around. The M16 had almost no recoil. It had a kick like a 22 rimfire. You could lie down in a hole and hold the 16 above you and shoot in the general direction of the enemy fire. Try that with an M-14 or Garand! This was not considered to be good technique.

When we went down the hill past the dead gook, we were told to stay back. He had been hit in the chest by a grenade from an M-79 grenade launcher. The round had not exploded, but he was dead anyway. Either it was a dud or the round had not traveled the prescribed 10 meters before it hit him. The engineer who devised the weapon knew the killing radius was 5 meters so he designed the gold grenade so it had to travel 10 meters before it went off. I heard of two other instances where dud golden eggs were embedded and the receivers lived. Once it was an NVA soldier and the other time an American. A few days later I was almost impaled with one of the egg shaped 40mm gold grenades just like the dead enemy I saw.

One day on Hill 714, Clarence was walking point when he spotted a wire across the trail. On closer investigation it was indeed a booby trap. The somewhat obvious wire was connected to a Chinese hand grenade. The hand grenade was inside of an old Charlie rat can nailed to a tree. If someone hit the wire, the grenade would be pulled out. It was somewhat of an amateurish set up, but could have been deadly. I don't remember if the fuse was instant or if it had a three-second delay like most grenades.

This was the only time that I saw a true booby trap in Nam. These devices could kill your own guys, too. The NVA unlike their Viet Cong cousins apparently didn't use many of these faceless killers. The possibility of a trap like this would also keep a point man's eyes down more often, making the unit more susceptible to ambushes. The point men on Hill 714 also had to watch for tree top warriors. They did use tree stands a few weeks later against Charlie Company.

As retaliation, we set up a homemade mechanical ambush that night about 100 yards uphill on a giant trail. Sometimes these were called widow-makers. A claymore was set in a direction that covered a good area on the trail. Instead of using the clacker, we borrowed a radio battery and made a circuit into the kill zone of the claymore. Two insulated electric wires with bare looped ends were mated together. When an enemy hit the trip wire the two wires would slide along each other until the bare loop ends met. The last thing done to complete the circuit was hooking up the battery, which was safely out of the kill zone.

In the middle of the night, the ambush went off. One of the line companies near us called to see what was going on and soon BN called also. I told them we would check it out in the morning. Come morning we slowly went up and found nothing. Apparently the wind or a critter had set it off. Soon BN called and asked for a report on what happened. I told them that we got a monkey. L.T. Hill gave me his famous glance and walked away with a grin. We didn't use mechanical ambushes as much as some units. We should have, but it was not Recons primary mission, and they required discipline and proper training. There were many sophisticated trip wire set-ups that we didn't have with us and you always had to go back and take it down if it didn't go off. There was also the danger of another American unit walking into it.

Chapter 39

FIGHTING ON HILL 714

The next skirmish on 714 started out with some dinks firing at Recon and Bravo. Several of us Recon guys managed to get in the prime middle positions of an on-line assault. Most civilians would think that the safest place in combat would be in a nice damp foxhole, but that's not true. Once you gained fire superiority and got their heads down, they were in real trouble. You could just walk up blazing and send them to commie hell. The only danger was sticking your head over a foxhole and looking in.

The other RTO in the Recon command post was a tall dorky guy like me. His M16 had jammed badly on this assault so he threw it down and grabbed a big club-like branch lying on the ground. He went in line with us facing automatic rifles and grenades with a stick for a weapon. There was some wisecracking going on during the close quarters combat. After the gooks were dispatched, L.T. Hill was shaking his head in disbelief. He told several of us, "You know! Slider has the biggest balls in the Army!" Ben had joined the legends of the Recon Platoon. Those guys at Ft. Carson were right; baseball bats would have been effective in very close combat. Well, at least after you got their heads down.

The gooks set up a line of foxholes 100 yards back from every line that we knocked out. The next line was just like the previous one. Somehow we managed to be in the middle of the assault again. This time one of the cornered dinks threw a grenade out of his hole at the last second about 10 feet to my right in front of L.T. Hill and several other Recon Guys. I remember someone shouting grenade and out of the side of my vision seeing one roll in front of my comrades. I was too busy with bunkers in front of me to see anymore. It's a scary feeling when you see a hand coming out of a hole holding a grenade that close to you.

L.T. Hill and three other Recondos were hit. L.T. Hill had a damaged arm and the other three guys had leg wounds. I felt the blast, but was not hit by any fragments. Our Battalion executive officer Major Hamby had come out to the scene of the battles with his cigar in one hand and a 45 pistol in the other. He managed to get hit with some of the grenade. There was no wisecracking when the grenade came out. At least the dink didn't get away. After the battle we looked at several of his grenades that failed to go off or weren't thrown. They were metal pipe ends or caps filled with explosive. The open end was plugged with a piece of wood with a small hole to the middle and the TNT. Pulling a pull string igniter, similar to what we called a pull-string booby trap in grade school, set it off. It was very primitive compared to our grenades. If the dink had had good grenades about five of us would have been dead.

L.T. Hill was gone for a few days. I found out later that one of the guys that was awarded a Purple Heart that day had jungle rot on his skin. When he went to the medic that day it was just assumed that it was caused by combat. There was some laughing a few days later about the jungle rot being a reason for a purple heart. There were many firefights during this period. Sometimes there were multiple slugfests in one day. The battles and incidents are a little blurry and intertwined.

Bravo Company handled the next row of bunkers nicely. After the battle, I was where they had found a supply depot. An

NVA soldier had been thrown head first into a foxhole. His legs pointed up out of a hole, which gave the impression of a giant peace sign. I guess some joker had a morbid sense of humor. Several ledger books were captured. The Battalion Vietnamese interpreter said that it was a list of everyone that was selling rice to the NVA. He also said that they would soon be in beaucoup trouble. What really irritated some of us was what was in their supply depot.

The enemy had all kinds of canned European hams and other non-perishable goods. Apparently a lot of countries believed the crocodile tears of the North Vietnamese about famine due to our bombing. They were sending food for the poor starving children and widows. Anything that would last the trip to the south was instead shunted to the NVA forces in the south. We did liberate some of the more premium treats and ate well that night. Another thing that bothered me was a recaptured American watch. Who did it belong to?

Many people might wonder what it is like to be in combat. I'm sure each individual reacts somewhat differently. In my case, I had much fear when combat was imminent the first few times. After a few firefights on Hill 714, my fear abated. During close combat I was too busy to actually react in the basic human instinct to stay alive. One of the reasons that I survived was that I went beyond two of the things that can get a soldier killed. One of them is excessive fear, which leads to an enemy killing you. The other is overzealous bravery. Charging machine guns that you have no chance of taking out and getting yourself killed serves no purpose. Devising a way to destroy the machine gun crew is what's important. The mission statement is "Close with and kill the enemy." Your job is to stop him and not to collect a Purple Heart medal to be sent to your family. The key to this is proper training, use of resources, and discipline. This is true for an individual or a group. I mention groups because in every war some poorly led units suffer more casualties than average. Thoughts and reaction to situations must be almost instantaneous. Combat is fast and furious in the jungle. There are no second chances.

Because of noise discipline, the jungle is always overly quiet before combat. The only thing that can be heard is the slight sound of boots on the path or backpacks shifting. If hiking up a steep hill or if combat is imminent, the sound of one's own heart can be heard. Then it happens—the first indication of combat. It might be a gunshot, or a loud explosion, or simply the visual recognition of the enemy. Instantly the mind and body go through a rapid metamorphosis into combat mode. An overwhelming adrenalin rush takes place. Within a millisecond the rifle is ready to fire. As soon as possible the backpack is jettisoned. The trained and experienced soldier is already reacting in a Pavlovian nature and starting to defend himself by trying to kill the enemy before the enemy kills him. The inexperienced soldier is either lucky or dead.

There is now a lot of noise, but the soldier may not even hear it. M16 rifles aimed out are very loud. AK-47s aimcd at him at close distances have an even louder, deafening clack clack clack. Occasionally, in the middle of this noise the loud ka boom of a grenade is heard. Sometimes the red flash of the enemy's rifle fire is seen, but usually smoke among the greenery is all that is seen. Leaves might be falling off the trees due to stray bullets, but the soldier doesn't notice. Sometimes the enemy is seen, but this is not often the case because he is acting like you, trying to hide to try to kill you. The smell of burnt gunpowder and explosives permeates the air. Occasionally a voice calling out an order or information is heard. Sometimes it is the moaning of a wounded soldier crying out, "Medic, medic."

Soon it is over. The enemy has either withdrawn or they are all dead. The adrenalin starts to come down. The experienced soldier is getting his combat gear in order. Collecting empty magazines and refilling them are a top priority. The RTOs are calling in a dustoff to get the wounded to the hospital. Officers are calling in SitReps and making sure their sergeants are bringing order out of confusion. The scene has a lot of subdued noise. For some, nothing is heard or experienced because they are looking at the bodies of the dead. Deep within their mind they are thinking that this still, and sometimes mutilated, body could have been them. Soon it is silent except for the soldier sighing as he goes back into grunt mode.

Chapter 40

DEATH ON A
YELLOW BRICK ROAD

The next day Recon was selected to go down what we sometimes called a yellow brick road. We had not gone too far when several AKs opened up on us on our right flank. There was an immediate counterattack that killed one of the attackers. The gooks were no longer digging in after their many losses the previous week. It was now hit and run. Since we were not with a line company, I had to stay with the radio. One of our guys was dead and two others wounded. I called in a medivac or dustoff as we called them on the radio and they were soon there. Recon had extended its perimeter to protect the medivac chopper with the bright red crosses. Things were getting very hectic.

The first time the basket was lowered I put a fellow Iowan in it. He had been hit multiple times with rifle fire. He was soon hoisted up and secured. His tour in Nam was done and I would run into him a year later in the states. They lowered the basket a second time for the other wounded guy. Panic set in as the other wounded guy could not be found and nobody knew where he was. He was soon found, but not before the man on the medivac yelled at me and threatened to leave. He had been over showing his million-dollar wound to his friends. We got him on the basket and he told me to go and kill all those damn gooks. Yeah, like I could single handedly clean these hills of NVA.

Medivacs sometimes take bodies out, but there was no room this trip. Some guys from the line company with us carried our fallen comrade all the way to the top of the hill the next day. Because of this, his official day of death is one day late in the records. They had set an ambush on the side of the trail. The point man was concentrating so much in front that he didn't see the enemy on the right side. I had just gotten to know Steve Sandlin a few days before. He was a real fine guy from California. This was the first time I saw the body of someone from Recon. The KIAs on FSB rifle were gone when we returned that day months ago. It was tough to take and I never got used to it. This time I was part of it. Luckily the gooks never shot down the Medivac. There was no chivalry in this war. No time outs to collect the dead. It was not the last time that I would see dead Recondos.

Combat on Hill 714 was almost a daily occurrence. Two days later on a calm clear morning, we were a little farther up a ridge. Twice in broad daylight, gooks dressed in wet weather ponchos trying to look like American grunts had walked down the trail like they owned the place. Both times they had gotten away because the guys on OP were fooled and shot too late. The OP position was a small foxhole with an ammo box filled with dirt ahead of it. I stupidly volunteered to man it for a while despite a lifelong problem with attention deficit disorder. The plan was to take careful aim and take care of the gook problem. A guy from the Associated Press had been with us a couple of times during the preceding week. He usually disappeared as soon as the bullets flew. He was back again, but nobody paid him any attention.

Chapter 41

ALL DOGS GO TO HEAVEN

They brought in a dog team to help out. One of the dogs, a fine looking German shepherd, was running around with the grunts having a good time and soon was next to me in the hole. I had a lot on my mind and could only play a little with him. He didn't like being ignored and left after a short time. Later the dog handler, Charlie Handler took over the hole with Danny his dog. The guy from the AP took a photograph. It was later an AP release. Some of the guys from Recon thought that it was a photo of me when it was published. I was probably cleaning my rifle getting ready for the impending combat that day. As they say, everyone has their fifteen minutes of fame and every dog has its day.

About an hour later Bravo Company and the remnants of Recon were told to get ready to move out. One squad of Recon was down on FSB Veghel and several wounded had not returned yet. Since I didn't have to handle the radio, I went with the troops. The dog and his trainer led. This was kind of silly since everyone knew there had to be gooks a short distance ahead. We followed on line about 8 feet behind and had gone only about 40 meters when the dog gave the alert signal. Within a millisecond, there was a loud ka-boom and the dog went down. The dog had his chest blown away. Everybody was very irate when Danny the Dog bit the dust on Hill 714.

Dogged Defense on Hill 714

A soldier of the U.S. 101st Airborne Div. stands watch with from Communist troops after four days of stiff fighting. Red a scout dog at a newly-erected bunker atop Hill 714, west of Hue forces on the hill had turned it into a honeycomb of bunkers and in northern South Vietnam. Members of the 101st took the hill other fortified positions. (AP)

Danny and Charlie Holder

Without any orders being given by the officers, the line of Recondos and Bravo guys laid down a torrent of bullets and walked up the ridge. Soon a row of foxholes was seen. All of a sudden, this gook stood up about 6 feet in front of me holding an M-79 American grenade launcher. He and all the gooks were dead in seconds. Had I been hit with the grenade launcher the round would not have exploded because I was too close to him. A 40mm hole would have hurt though. The mass of troopers continued on for about 100 yards before all firing stopped.

A strange sensation came over me when I looked down and saw a small songbird with his wing shot off. I thought of the movie version of *All Quiet on the Western Front* where Paul Baumer reaches out to touch the flower and gets nailed by the Tommy sniper. A similar scene is also in the movie version of *The Naked and the Dead* where a soldier finds a wounded bird. I sobered up quickly and humanely stepped on the bird. Carney's words came back to me — "stay alert and never lose your concentration in Nam." There were about fifty guys spread out all along the ridge. Some were laughing about the turkey shoot.

131

A chopper flew over and dropped a case of 5.56 M16 ammo since some guys had emptied all their magazines. There were magazines lying all over and I picked a few up to replenish my depleted stock from the previous week. I was worried about the flanks and yelled to a couple of guys to watch the other side. The NVA could have come up the flanks and nailed us good. I slowly walked back to the starting point thinking about life and death. When the bunkers were reached I liberated the dog killer of his helmet, shirt, and belt buckle as trophies. His name was on the inside, Vinh, and I kept his helmet for twenty-five years. In addition we recaptured a lot of American equipment including two working prick 25 radios. Where did these guys get this stuff? Maybe the "grenades from the treetops" story was true?

A little farther on the ridge I stopped by the handler and his dog. They were in a time of communion. The soldier was mourning the loss of his closest companion that had just given his life to save a bunch of us. I tried to tell him how sorry I was about the dog, but he didn't hear me.

Doc Ackerman then came up to me and said, "Let me see your leg Jim." My leg was bleeding and I didn't even know it. My fatigue bottoms were removed and Doc removed several small fragments from my legs and cleaned a few other cuts. There was a small wound between my fingers also. Thimerosal and Band-Aides took care of the problem. "Drive on trooper, but let me know if you have any problems." I was the only guy wounded that day that I know of and have the right to say that I am a blood brother of German Shepherd dogs.

Ironically, an American weapon in the hands of an NVA soldier hit me. I was totally immune to NVA bullets my whole nine months in the jungle. It wasn't because I was a poor target. I am 6' 3" tall. Perhaps I was skinny enough in those days that I could lay rather low when I had to.

Chapter 42

HOT DOG RIDGE
AND KENT STATE

A little later some guy from Bravo Company had erected a sign from a Charlie rat box that said "Welcome to Hot Dog Ridge." Grunts in Korea and Viet Nam had a tendency to name every hill or ridge. Charlie Company soon showed up and took over for Bravo and Recon. They moved up the trail a bit and the point man turned white with fright. A gun muzzle was sticking out at him from a pile of brush, but nothing happened. The gooks had hastily tried to hide a large pile of weapons. Included were many sniper rifles and old French Sub-machine guns that probably had a history going back to 1954. I remember comments about how Bravo and Recon had done all the work and the Charlie guys would get all the trophies to take home. A lot of Brass came out and there was a photo session and pats on the back. This was the last time we would see Charlie Company for three weeks. The next time we saw them they would be platoon sized.

About this time a tragedy happened back in the states. Four students were killed at Kent State. We were very busy in combat, but still comments were made. Some wanted to go back and clean out the campuses and others said the students were just trying to get us back home alive. Ironically one of the students killed was an ROTC student that got in the way. The homefront was divided. No one out in the jungle was throwing down their weapons and refusing to fight. The one thing we all had in common was a lack of respect for NGs.

This was all precipitated by the US invasion of Cambodia a few days before. The US press, as usual, made a big deal out of the Cambodia invasion when the most intense battles of the year took place much to the north in the jungles west of Hue from April to September. Some of us were hoping that the US forces would head north out of Cambodia, into Laos, and meet us in the A Shau valley. I'm sure it crossed someone's mind in the General Staff.

Chapter 43

CON MEN

We were soon sent on another mission. We were sent to secure an LZ on an old FSB. It was on a high knob with a spectacular view. I believe it was to protect a Huey that was hit and made an Emergency landing. A CH-47 Chinook came and picked it up. We had been in combat on a daily basis for about ten days and this brief stint away from the fighting had our minds spinning. L.T. Hill was still gone due to his wound and Platoon Sergeant Jeff "Pappy" Yocom was in charge. We were a light Platoon due to death and injuries and some Recondos were still helping out at the firebase.

Jeffrey "Pappy" Yocum at Company E Bar

After the chopper was lifted out Pappy and I had a little conference. It was late afternoon and we had no orders. We were several clicks from any other Strike Force guys and it was all Indian country in between. This country was very dangerous for small units to operate. They had probably forgotten about us on the old abandoned FSB. I got on the radio and called Battalion. The message I gave was real simple. I said that we were on the LZ and we had no orders. What should we do? The guy at the other end said to come back to Camp Eagle and I told him we needed some Slicks ASAP, since it would be dark soon. It was a great feeling being lifted out of that country. We had the feeling that the battle was over. This of course was misguided optimism. The Battalion had fared well up to now with very few casualties and lots of dead NVA. Despite losing one man and having some wounded we were still very cocky. When we arrived at the heliport above the BN area CSM Sabalauski met us and congratulated us. He also asked us what we were doing at Camp Eagle. Since he didn't know we were coming in, he didn't have a barbershop set up for us.

We were the epitome of the expression grunt. It was suppertime and we all went down to the mess hall for what seemed like the best meal of my life. Eating had been very inconsistent the past couple of weeks and my body frame was getting thinner. All of a sudden, the cooks and the other REMFs started yelling and congratulating us. We were heroes to them. They let us go through the chow line first. Thinking back on the whole experience in Nam, this was the only substantial thanks that I ever received from a non-relative. We were soon accosted by the BN XO who wondered why we were there and who gave authorization for us to be there. Pappy and I, with innocent looks on our faces, told him how we had asked for orders and were told to come in. If L.T. Hill had been at S2 meeting, I'm sure they would have found a better task. It took them about a day, but they did. We had weaseled our way into the rear and were real proud of ourselves.

L.T. Hill was soon back with us and we had a little conference on our next mission. Just northeast of Hill 714 was another hill elevation 882 named Dong Kein Kein. Hill 882 was

136

next to the Song Bo River, which headed north and east out toward the Hue area. Anytime I see the numbers 714 or 882 flashbacks still occur to me. Sgt. Joe Friday's badge number 714 on *Dragnet* would even rekindle memories.

The mission was simple. Two squads of Recon were to rappel out of Hueys onto the top of Hill 882 and secure the top while engineers rappelled down. They were going to blow an LZ on this previously unexplored hill. The guys immediately balked and started arguing with L.T. Hill. These were experienced, battle-hardened grunts who had risked their lives many times before and this seemed like a suicide mission. That was dangerous country out there to be sliding down a rope out of a chopper. The one night back in the rear had given guys a little time to become fearful again. This went on for ten minutes with L.T. trying to convince us to go.

Finally one of our old time guys that didn't have the best reputation as a soldier stepped forward and said, "These guys are going to get us all killed anyway. It might as well be today." The Recondos then all marched up the heliport wisecracking to each other about writing letters home if they "buy the ranch." One guy told another he would look his girlfriend up. The soldier's prophecy was very accurate.

Chapter 44

HILL 882 – DANGER RISING

At first everything went very well. The hilltop had been extensively blasted by artillery. This always helped keep the dinks heads down, but also told all the bad guys that the Strike Force was coming. Both Recon squads got down with only one minor injury. One guy hit his rear on a broken tree. After the Recon squads were down the engineers from the 326th Engineering BN started to come down their ropes. Despite a perimeter having been set up, some gooks fired up at the engineer's chopper. It made it out, but was crippled by the attack. The engineers had the explosives dropped and soon began to blow a very large LZ. It was very obvious that the dinks didn't like an LZ blasted on this hilltop. We all knew that trouble was nearby. Just like over on Hill 714 there was a yellow brick road leading down hill.

Recon was selected to go first and check out Hill 882. We started down the trail, which soon grew wider. The entire top of the ridge was flat and the width of a narrow two-lane road, and it dropped off very sharply at both sides. We were all very tense because this was a scary place plus we stopped frequently to look around. A gook started to come up over the side to take a shot at us. One of our guys, "Okie," was very alert and shot at the gook that was about 6 feet away. He didn't know if he got him, but he rolled back down the side of the ridge.

Less than a minute later, the strangest thing that I ever saw in Nam happened. Another gook crawled up and let go a single shot. It hit a grenade that was on the web belt of a short stocky Sancho Panza-looking guy named Pablo. The grenade started to smoke and we all dove in different directions. We were all trying to save ourselves, yet Pablo, with great dexterity, got the grenade off and heaved it over the side of the ridge where it did no harm. We were surrounded and they were closing in for the kill. Pablo was so shaken up that as soon as he could, he took a three-year enlistment to get out of the field.

I called in a situation report for the L.T. and we were told to hold up. The L.T. was busy telling guys to be cool and to set up a defensive perimeter. Help was on the way. I had this feeling we were all going to be goners in a moment. This place, like 714, was too dangerous to be out in platoon strength.

Battles were still being fought over on Hill 714. Charlie Company was paying dearly for finding the weapons. The NVA even tried using their tree stands again. Alpha Company had also hit some bad stuff going the other way from the top of Hill 882.

Obtaining water was always a problem up on the mountain. If you walk 100 meters down toward a stream you would be sure to be in a firefight. One afternoon we went to the top of Hill 882 to fill our canteens. The choppers came down close to the ground and artillery canisters filled with foul, gunpowder-tasting water were dropped. I looked up at the pilot and saw Jim Walter, my bunkmate from Basic Training, hovering. I gave him a wave and he nodded his head back. All those months and miles and we ended up at the same stinking place.

Alpha Company soon joined us and things were not as bad as they seemed for a few days. For the next few weeks we were often attached to them. This was good and bad. Even a well-disciplined line company when it is operating together is hard to conceal. We were with them and I'm sure some dink Colonel had us on his TOC map every night and was complaining about us being in his backyard. We started battling down the hill.

A couple of days later, a Platoon of Alpha attacked three lines of bunkers nearby and took some casualties. There is a feeling of power when you are with a large group in a combat situation. Alpha stayed two nights in one NDP. I spent both nights in a very large foxhole originally built by the gooks. On the third night L.T. Hill got permission to set Recon up about 150 yards down the hill. This was a risky move, but it was good luck for Recon. We sneaked out in the late afternoon and set up a small tight perimeter. It seemed dangerous, but it probably saved my life.

Chapter 45

BLOOD AND GUTS

I remember this site and this night very well. There was a large evergreen tree on top of the ridge where we set up our CP. This was the only conifer I ever saw in Nam. Roots and rocks made it impossible to stretch out and sleep. I was back on the radio because we were separate from Alpha. It was a cold, rainy night for this time of the year in the tropics. I shivered so hard my teeth were near chattering. A series of explosions started up at Alpha early the next morning. They were under attack. This went on for what seemed like an eternity. The grunts were firing back with rifles. We were close by, but the trees kept anything from getting to us. I was monitoring the radio and knew that Alpha had five men dead.

I was whispering SitReps to L.T. Hill and he was whispering to the guys. He had everyone in a defensive posture. Soon it was silent up above us. All of a sudden this gook started talking on the Battalion frequency in broken English bragging about what they just did. I said, "F**k you gook" on the radio. Then L.T. Hill gave me a glance to shut up. Dawn slowly came and there was a loud explosion right at the edge of our perimeter towards Alpha. L.T. Hill in a low voice asked what was going on. One of our old timers who only had a few days left in the field whispered back that he set off his claymore mine on a gook. The claymore was set at an upward angle and the blast was deafening. The gook was moaning on the trail with the lower half of his body completely blown off. He wouldn't die and just kept moaning for what seemed forever. I kept thinking over and over "Die! Die!" because I couldn't stand to hear him. Finally he was quiet. We waited quietly and I whispered a SitRep to BN. About ten minutes later, a second gook walked right into our perimeter. The last thing he saw was his mutilated comrade lying on the trail. About ten minutes later another one walked right into us. He too was dispatched. Our old timer had killed, or helped kill, three gooks shortly before he went home. A few days later he was probably having supper with his family in the Southland. No more gooks came down the trail. All three were toting RPGs. We collected all their equipment and went back up to Alpha Company.

Things were very sullen up at their location. They had lost four men plus a guy from Headquarters Company. A Staff Sergeant was killed in the large foxhole that I had been in the night before. I started wondering how much longer my luck would hold out. I had missed the action at FSB Rifle and now I missed this fiasco. Some brass came in and analyzed what had happened. They pointed out that the company had stayed too long in one spot. Staying in an area under a copse of trees with open areas around would make you a corpse. The last thing noted was that all return fire was 6 to 8 feet off the ground. In their panic they shot straight out forgetting that the hill dropped off rather acutely. The brass usually had an after action report for every incident. The information learned was put into what was called Lessons Learned Reports and given to commanders. Alpha Company would do much better next time.

The hills west of Hue were covered with leaflets dropped by the military's Psychological Operations Section. The pamphlets told the North Vietnamese exactly how they could save their lives by coming over to the RVN side. The program was set up for the Viet Cong and many took advantage of the open door policy. The NVA came from hundreds of miles to the north, and if they deserted they were leaving their whole world behind. I saw one demonstrate how to crawl through wire back at FSB Rifle.

On Hill 714, I even picked up a leaflet telling me how I could do the same. It was cute. It contained very British English. It is now in my photo album of Nam. In 1975, these guys that came over to the Republic of Viet Nam side were in real danger. Our Battalion interpreter did make it out of Nam, but his family was split. The only psychological method used by Recon was the frequent nailing of *Playboy* centerfolds to trees. I really don't know what this was supposed to accomplish.

THE SOUTH VIETNAM NATIONAL FRONT FOR LIBERATION GIVES LENIENT AND HUMANE TREATMENT TO RALL'ED ARMYMEN AND PRISONERS-OF-WAR

« To welcome puppet officers and soldiers and puppet officials back to the just cause ; show leniency and give humane treatment to rallied armymen and prisoners-of-war.

☆ Captured officers and soldiers of the puppet army will enjoy humane treatment and leniency,

☆ Men in the US army and its satellite armies who cross over to the peoples side will be given kind treatment and helped to return to their families when conditions permit.

☆ Captured U.S. and satellite troops will receive the same treatment as captured puppet troops... »

(Article 12 of the SVNNFL'S Political programme)

HOW TO SURRENDER OR TO CROSS OVER TO THE NFL's SIDE

— Gun on the ground or slung across the back

— Hands up above the head

— If still at some distance from the Liberation troops, tie a white cloth to the tip of your gun.

CÁCH ĐẦU HÀNG HOẶC KHI CHẠY SANG PHÍA MẶT TRẬN D.T.G.P.

— Bỏ súng xuống đất hoặc khoác chéo sau lưng.

— Dơ tay cao quá đầu.

— Nếu còn cách xa quân Giải phóng, buộc một mảnh vải trắng vào đầu súng.

 Truyền đơn giặc thích chính sách tù hàng binh dành cho binh sĩ Mỹ.

NVA surrender pamphlet

143

Chapter 46

CHERRY TO HARDCORE

Both Alpha and Recon soon had replacements come in. These were cherries or sometimes called FNGs and they had it rough. It is very tough to go out to a hilltop, jump off a chopper, and throw some body bags back on. This happened to a replacement from my home state of Iowa on Hill 882. After helping unload a chopper he had the task of putting full body bags back on the same chopper. Someone told him to go over and guard the perimeter. This guy then told him, "Keep alert or you will end up in one these."

Another new guy later told me a similar story of how difficult it is to know you are replacing a dead guy. I had it easy when I came out compared to these guys. His next job even before he linked up with Recon was to help dig up some NVA bodies and get information from them. What a welcome to Viet Nam.

A few days later we got into a skirmish and this new guy hit close to a gook with an M-79 grenade round. There was blood on the stump that the gook was hiding behind. He started complaining that he didn't have a body to show for his work. He was told that the dink would die if he had any holes in his lungs.

The new guy was still upset. In the middle of this, a wisecrack was made about how you can't take them home and mount them on the wall. The new guy didn't hear this crack, but it wouldn't have fazed him any. He was already hardcore, no longer a cherry. Recon was already a vastly different unit from the one I first linked up with in December.

One time months later, we had received another cocky cherry within Recon. He found out that I was the FO in addition to RTO. He then started to question my ability to call in arty. In the open valley, there was a lonely tree. I called up the BN CP and asked if I could do a little arty practice. Surprisingly enough it wasn't a problem. Seconds later, the sound of 81mm mortars were heard. I used the compass and map, and the first round dropped about 10 meters to the right and 10 meters high. I adjusted and dropped the second round on top of the tree.

Someone said that if there was an NVA spotter in the tree he would have soiled his pants the first round and died the second. I was real proud of myself. The cherry asked if he could try it. We picked out another tree and the new kid on the block also hit his tree by the second shot. Damn, the rookie was as good as me. It was a humbling experience. I then gave him some advice about shooting by sound and not by sight. To save face, I challenged him again, suggesting that we do the same thing blindfolded. Common sense prevailed, the contest was ended, and I was somewhat satisfied. The only thought in my mind was "damn cherry."

Bob Cain was another FNG. He was one of the few new guys who I found interesting. He never seemed afraid of anything. He was, however, concerned that he might have to shoot women and children. He jokingly said, "I'm a baby killer, I'm a baby killer." I didn't take him completely seriously. He was just repeating what the anti-war crowd was saying. They and the Mai Lai massacre had made soldiers something to mock. Apparently someone had called Bob a baby killer on the homefront. Several others and I talked with him for a while. New guys that didn't talk had to be watched over.

The next skirmish was a running firefight. As usual, I was near the front when it started. I saw a gook stand up to run.

Some Alpha guys slightly ahead of me opened up and started chasing him and one of his pals. One Alpha guy let go a burst and I saw him hit another Alpha guy in the leg about 10 feet ahead of me. The injured guy yelled back, "You shot me!" The other guy vehemently denied it. Years later, I found out from another Alpha guy that he saw a similar incident the same day. They were chasing a couple of trail watchers and wounded two of their own. The day was May 19th, yet we had been in almost continuous combat since April 24th. The gooks were not giving up this second hill without a fight.

That evening Recon slipped away from Alpha again, this time probably about 75 yards. There wasn't enough room on the ridge and maybe we could fool the gooks again by setting up away from Alpha. Like clockwork, Alpha was hit again, but this time, they did splendidly. The location was better and they were ready with a list of new tricks. No one was killed, although a few were wounded.

At morning, we moved back up with them. No gooks had run down into our positions. Alpha might have gotten them all. Two Alpha guys had dug a foxhole right behind a giant Eucalyptus tree. They had buried a claymore underground pointed up at an angle at the other side. As soon as the action started, they set it off. Some dinks had positioned themselves right behind the tree hoping to have a safe place to do a lot of damage. They were blown to pieces. The two Alpha guys were still standing in the foxhole filled with water.

I was standing around looking the scene over and the two grunts were asked to get a body count. They had a slight perplexed look on their faces. I joined in and helped them. We soon figured out that there were three dead dinks after laying some of the pieces back together. Dr. Hick's anatomy lessons at Iowa State University had come in handy again. The three enemies had probably felt around looking for a claymore, but found only earth.

One of the gooks was carrying a wallet. Inside of it were some family photos and Catholic holy pictures, and this bothered me a little. Another one had a card that our interpreter said was an award for killing a GI. Another had a pen that said Hanoi and a propaganda stamp in his green uniform. I went over to talk to a wounded Alpha guy. He was very sullen. Another Alpha guy came over and asked if it was true that he was hit in the crotch. The reply was, "Yeah. And it's not very funny." This whole action is missing from the BN record. It was a miserable foggy morning, when L.T. Hill told us that Recon was going to take the lead today. We were up to full strength with the addition of several FNGs (F**king New Guys).

Chapter 47

FOGGY DOOM

It was May 20th, the longest day of my life. We were caught in the thickest fog we had ever seen. The troops in Nam had several advantages over the NVA, such as air support. A thick fog stopped the use of attack helicopters and even jets. Morale was better than in previous wars because the hospital was only a half-hour away by medivac helicopter. That wasn't what worried us.

What did worry us was that we were bluntly told that the dinks would probably be waiting for us. We already knew that, since you couldn't walk 100 meters in the area without getting into a firefight. It was the same kind of ridge that was common up there. It was flat on top with a steep drop off on both sides and perfect for funneling grunts into an ambush.

Our point man stopped us several times to confer with the L.T. and also to examine footprints and tree markings. The ridge dropped into a slight saddle and then started to rise up again. The fog got even thicker. All this damn fog wasn't helping at all. Suddenly the point man shot a burst of bullets at a lone gook probably no more than 15 feet ahead. The L.T. hollered, "What's going on?" and he got a report. The first squad started to move into combat mode by starting a line. Before that was completed a battle started up. Our M-60 machine gun team of Gary Gear and Bob Cain started to move forward spraying the area ahead of them. It looked as if we were up to our old tricks. We had not only broken the enemy ambush by discovering their position first, but we also had fire superiority and were closing in for the mop up. These techniques had worked well in the previous weeks. Gary and Bob were almost at the bunkers shooting away like the team of John Wayne and Audie Murphy.

I was walking about 10 feet behind the 60 team when a loud explosion went off. Before I realized what happened, Gary and Bob went down and an RPD machine gun started opening up on us. All of the first squad went down under the stream of bullets from the machine gun. The L.T. said to me, "Get going Jim!" I took off with a lifer Sergeant replacement who had never seen combat. We went slightly to the left by Gary and Bob who were both alive and lucid. Gary even pointed the way and gave some encouragement. Right in front of us were three bunkers with dry palm leaves to conceal them. I started yelling like crazy for guys to come up and help out. A high school cheerleader couldn't have done better. I started to lose it just like Bob and Gary did a minute before.

I pointed out the camouflaged bunkers to the lifer FNG. We started to crawl up on the bunkers when the enemy with the RPD machine gun shot over us. This was on-the-job training at its best. I told the new guy to pull the pin on the grenade, release the handle, count one thousand one, one thousand two, and drop it in the nearest bunker while I covered him, but the guy refused. I told him that if he didn't do as I said, the dink would throw it back out. We called this technique cooking off grenades. I started to put my plan into action. Since I was the new guy's cover, I began popping rounds at the top of the bunkers to try to keep any heads down. The new guy systematically dropped three grenades down three holes. Finally we were getting somewhere!

Every now and then, I fired blindly to the right at the gook with the machine gun or at his comrade who was straight ahead of us. They returned fire in the form of large bursts just inches over our backs. The situation wasn't looking hopeful and

149

as it turned out only one of the holes was occupied. The new guy and I wasted a lot of time on two empty holes and the last of our grenades were tossed at the unseen enemy not far from us. We started over the top of the ridge just as L.T. Hill led the remaining Recon guys on the other side of the front. The NVA soldier with the machine gun had gotten away, but he left his RPD machine gun with six empty 100 round canisters. His commander was probably upset later because of this loss.

By then the Alpha guys took charge and began their chase on the gooks. I was happy to be alive, but I couldn't believe that the enemy escaped. I had nothing left to give; the shootout at high noon had totally drained me. So I stopped to look at our gook. I pulled him out of his hole and all his brains fell out on the ground. It was time for another anatomy lesson. I pointed out to several Recondos the various parts of the human brain such as cerebellum, cortex, hypothalamus, etc. One of my nicknames in Recon was Bugman because I frequently gave boring biology lessons. I had become totally hardcore, and, unfortunately, this scene became part of the legend of the Recon Platoon. I was no longer a nice innocent farm boy from the heartland.

After the battle, Docs Moreau and Ackerman worked on Gary and Bob. They looked much worse than before. Originally I thought they only had slight wounds. The medics had both rushed in facing the machine gun fire to help our wounded. These two were the bravest of the brave.

As I left the medics to continue their work on Bob and Gary, I discovered that one of the new guys, Claggett, was dead. He died instantly, and I hadn't even noticed him being shot down. The Alpha RTO had called in the dustoff and they were due soon. Quite a few others guys had been hit either by the pellets from the Chinese claymore or the RPDs bullets. The point man, Bob Childers, had survived with minor wounds, but had run out of ammo. A guy behind him had frozen and couldn't even throw some magazines up to him. I don't know if it was true, but I was told that my old harasser from many months before just hid behind a tree. L.T. Hill and the remnants of Recon had moved up into the jaws of death and had chased the gooks away.

A strange scene had developed earlier. Bob Childers was out of ammo as was the NVA manning the RPD. The dink had a second empty weapon and they both pointed their empty guns at each other until the gook fled. I took over handling the medivac call from the Alpha RTO when he moved up with his company. The medivac soon arrived in the general area, but all of Hill 882 was still covered with clouds. Medivacs had a tracking device that could hone in on the calling frequency when I was talking to them. We could hear them, but they never got close enough to see the lift basket. We kept trying for forty-five minutes. They soon had to leave to refuel. The fog was still very thick and it was mid afternoon.

I went back to Doc Moreau and found out that Gary was dead. Earlier, Gary told the guys he had his million dollar wound and was going home.

Chapter 48

WOUNDED WARRIORS

Bob was still bravely hanging on. He knew he was dying, but didn't once complain. He only mentioned that it was hard to breathe. A group of us gathered around to give him encouragement. Doc Moreau was yelling at Bob to think of his girlfriend and his family and hang on. Bob had only been with us a few days, but he was already our Brother. One guy was praying and another crossed himself. If only this fog would lift we thought. He was still with us, but then started to fail.

Doc had connected our last IV bottle, but it didn't do any good. Doc tried resuscitation, but it didn't work. Bob slowly faded away. His face had turned white from the loss of blood. Nothing the Doc did worked. We were all in shock. Three were dead and most of the rest of us were hit. Despite being right up there within touching distance of the enemy, I remained unscathed. Fate is often strange.

A second Chinese claymore was still set up at the ambush site. It had not gone off and was aimed in the direction where I stood earlier. Their claymores looked like large green pie dishes. This one was useless because Gary and Bob's 60 rounds had cut through the detonation wire when they sprayed the area before they were hit. The claymore had my name written all over it.

After Bob died we all sat around for a while. Bob Cain didn't have to worry about ever being a baby killer. There were no women and children around. A Communist regular killed him far from his home in the north.

I started to reflect and realized that I had crossed the line long ago. The question was not if I was going to make it, but rather when and how it would happen. I knew that the guys of Recon would drag my wounded or dead body back somehow. I started to get bloodthirsty and totally fearless, which had never been in my character before. Now it remained embedded in me like a huge war scar.

Some of the guys were sitting in pain, but none of them even whimpered. We were out of morphine, and in a few hours they would start to feel real pain. Ben Slider lost two fingers while pouring gun oil down his red-hot M16 barrel trying to cool it down. The round in the chamber got so hot it went off. The two fingers went flying up into the trees. This was also called cooking off. I had only heard of it happening with M-60 machine guns, although guys said that they saw M16s glow in the nighttime. There was a lot of lead thrown by both sides that day. Herschell "Okie" Martin had lost fingers and was also hit in the foot. Dave Hepburn lost an eye. Bob Hagemann and others also had various wounds. They and the other wounded sat by the dead that night in a silent vigil.

Recon was down to a squad of healthy guys. Alpha set up a perimeter for the night because the fog was still thick and wounded couldn't get out of the area. Volunteers were requested to set up a listening post about 100 feet from the perimeter right on the main trail. Chuck Kinsey, a fellow Iowan, another guy, and I volunteered and traveled at dusk to set up some claymores and to wait behind a large log. At dawn, we set off the claymores and came back in. Some of the wounded were really hurting, since all the effects of morphine had worn off. They were a brave bunch, but by mid-morning they were gone. I never really buddied up to any of their replacements. Only a few of the guys I knew in December were still here. Seven were dead and it was

153

impossible to count all the wounded that had left and never returned since February.

Captain Asher of E CO even got killed when the firebase was hit a few weeks before. He stepped out of his bunker to look after his men during a mortar attack. We had not even met him. Most of the combat during the previous month was unknown to the world because the press had its focus on the invasion of Cambodia and the Kent State fiasco. The 101st also didn't publicize casualties after all the bad press received one year earlier at a place the GIs dubbed Hamburger Hill.

That day, the last of the wounded were finally medivaced. A light observation helicopter was shot up checking the trail farther down. This of course meant the gooks were waiting for us again. It managed to land in a small emergency LZ that A Company had made a few days earlier. The chopper had some bullet holes in the rotors. It normally would have been fun to inspect the mini gun up close. Some guys started to touch it and were told not to turn the barrels. They were mechanically driven and could have started popping rounds.

The gooks were protecting something between Hills 714 and 882. Recon and A company had been fighting down Hill 882 and C Company had been doing the same coming down Hill 714. We would link up eventually. I was walking around in a state of shock. The often used comment "It don't mean nothing" would have got someone killed. It did mean something. None of us were very talkative that day; we were all just sad. Others were worse off than me. Encouragement didn't help much. Recon was down to squad size. L.T. Hill came to me and asked if I would be a squad leader and I was fine with that. It didn't happen because he left us a few days later. He also told me that he had put me in for the Silver Star, but was told by Battalion that too many had been given out to the dead guys. It didn't really matter to me. In less than a month, I had won three Bronze Stars for valor, which didn't mean anything to me either. I still had six months left to win a Silver Star, or to go home wounded or in a body bag

Medals for valor are supposed to be given only when a serviceman did something above what is expected. This is, of course, somewhat subjective. What is normal duty? A serviceman who plans on getting medals is really not doing his job. The mission is to close with and kill the enemy, not to put oneself in unnecessary jeopardy. Trying to get medals means throwing one's life away without taking out the foe. Of course, God or fate may intervene and both objectives are accomplished.

We had a young man come to our BN from another unit that had boasted to them that he was going to get a lot of hardware for his chest. They didn't want him with them because of this and other problems. Within a few weeks he died a hero's death and was buried with his medals.

Many a grunt suffered a full year or more in the worst of jungle warfare and never received any awards for valor. He simply did his job and killed the enemy before they killed him.

It is very possible that anyone reading my story will think that he had it much rougher than me. I salute these guys. They were among the unheralded grunts, heroes known only to themselves and the Almighty.

This is why the Combat Infantryman's Badge was started in WWII. It honors infantrymen who just showed up and did their job. In one of his speeches, General Hill said that this badge is the most meaningful emblem. Of my medals and awards, I value the CIB most highly.

Chapter 49

REUNIONS

I had not seen Charlie Company since they passed through Bravo and Recon on April 29th and found the big cache of weapons. During that time, they had seen combat on a routine basis. At one point, they had no more medics because all of them were either dead or wounded. One of our medics, Doc Ackerman had volunteered to rappel into their position to tend to some of the seriously wounded. The brass nixed the idea because it was too risky. It would have taken tremendous bravery to perform such an act.

I will never forget the look of Charlie Company being lead in by big Sgt. John Roberts. There weren't many of them, and they were very sullen. The combined total of men in Alpha, Charlie, and Recon that linked up was equivalent to a single full strength company. The 2/502 Infantry Battalion had lost thirty men in the past month. Four of them were from Recon. There were many wounded and many had not returned. Two guys from another BN attached to us were even killed on the firebase when a box of munitions they were carrying exploded. The angel of death seemed to be everywhere.

The next day we received three more FNGs. It is always tough on new guys when they are going into battle immediately after reaching the front because they are extremely nervous. They only had a few hours to acclimatize with us before the noise started. Early in the morning what was called a time-on-target started. It had become very obvious that something between the twin hills was important to some NVA commander. Almost in unison every artillery piece within range started hitting the knob between the hills. We were very close to the impact area and the noise was deafening. To me, the sound of our artillery working on the enemy was a wonderful sound. It was like all the Fourth of July's of my life rolled into one.

Most of the other old timers felt the same. We didn't want to walk into another kill zone. One of the new guys was suddenly having the shakes. He started shivering and then turned stiff from the tension. We all tried to tell him not to worry because it was our stuff being thrown at them. After a while of encouragement, he got a little better. It wasn't a sign of cowardliness, just a condition of shell shock. The human mind and body can only take so much. The bombardment lasted a few hours and it took a while for this guy to reach some sort of normalcy. He was a good soldier after that with a very subtle sense of humor. At dawn, the hodgepodge of battle weary grunts walked down into the knob area. The men were near breaking.

We walked into a wasteland of destroyed jungle. Soon we were in a base camp that had been destroyed by arty and hardly any tree was left standing. It looked like a large salad of tangled leaves and twigs. Arty had hit right on target. Both aerial and delayed fuse rounds had been used. The delayed fuse rounds went off deep in the ground collapsing bunkers. The survivors had removed their dead and some older bodies were found that they had died of small arms fire from the previous few days fighting. I have always wondered who wasted these gooks. More bodies were probably buried in the collapsed bunkers.

All kinds of armament was scattered about. Some of the guys from a line company got a little out of control. The month of combat and the loss of so many buddies made them forget their professionalism. Three dead NVA soldiers were propped up

157

against trees with their helmets on and cigarettes in their mouths. Their hands were placed in their shorts as if they were playing with themselves. Widowmaker cards were left with all of them and then left for their comrades to find. Some of these guys even took photos of the dead in their unflattering poses. This scene unfortunately became part of Strike Force lore and was included in a book.

An officer made a comment that no ears would be collected for boony-rat necklaces. The rest of the morning was spent collecting armament. We decided to make a big pile and blow it in place. These guys even had anti-tank mines. I picked up a real nice AK-47. It was Russian built and even had a plastic pistol grip. I knew that I couldn't take it home, but it was so nice I decided to keep it awhile. I was immediately called Two Gun by some of my wiseass comrades. I wanted to shoot it sometime to experience a Kalashnikov, but I never got the opportunity.

I took a complete NVA uniform including a prized NVA officer's belt with a red star on it back to the rear. This included a helmet and a North Vietnamese fatigue top with K-7 Battalion embroidered on. I even collected a pair of Ho Chi Minh racing slicks or tire tread sandals. A few years later these became very popular in the USA. No doubt some Veteran brought the idea back from Nam. Other items that I collected were two hand-forged machetes with palm wood handles. My backpack was full.

A few days later, we were all pulled out of the area and traded places with the 1/327 BN. We thought that we had cleaned the whole area of NVA. They ran into the same troubles that we did when they started to head north off of Hill 882. Bravo Company of the 1/327 eventually found a sappers training camp with concertina wire to practice crawling through. They hit the same meat grinder. The battle for the area continued after we left. We were to be re-equipped, reinforced and retrained. I was half way through with my tour in Nam. What was the second half of my year going to be like? I was eligible to take a week and go on R&R.

Chapter 50

NEW L.T.s

We soon had a new L.T. He came with a good reputation and was even a graduate of the Recondo School in Ft. Carson. He knew his soldiering, but not how to get along with the Colonel. Every afternoon, S2/S3 would have a meeting and place the little map tacks on the board to show where everyone was located. We were often on the move and it upset him to give his location this time of day just so S2/S3 could have a nice meeting. Several of us told him just give your location at 3 p.m. and call in the change, if any, for the NDP.

The Colonel also got upset when one time we triangulated our 3 p.m. position by using two artillery bursts on click corners. Things kept on going downhill. A few of us old-timers kept telling him he was going to get in trouble. Even my old nemesis tried to give him some good fatherly advice, which seemed out of character. Sure enough after about two weeks of this cat and mouse stuff, they flew in a new L.T. and sent the other one to a line company. If he had only listened to his Sergeants, he would have done fine. The next L.T. was Dan Johnston and he would be with Recon for quite a few months. He always talked in whispers and was hard to hear. I didn't realize then that some of my hearing ability had been lost in the previous months.

Apparently the Colonel thought that we were out of shape after goofing off for a few weeks and had the new L.T. take us on a rigorous walk. Hard humps, or fast patrols, in the jungle were very hard and dangerous on the point man. None of us dropped out, and the area was relatively safe. We even got a lecture on how we should always wear a T-shirt under our jungle fatigues to keep cooler. He got some argument that not everything the Army told you was true and the subject was dropped. We soon had our new L.T. broken in.

A few days before I left for R&R, a new medic came out to us on re-supply. When the choppers came back an hour later he jumped back on. We were all disgusted at this state of cowardliness exhibited by a guy that had been sent to save lives. Unknown to us, this guy was real dangerous. He would later ruin a night's sleep for me. The same chopper brought in a guy that had only a few days left in Nam. Apparently he was such a discipline problem on the FSB that Captain Ciccolella sent him out to Recon for R&R. I don't remember him acting up out there in the bush. He probably thought that he had been sent out to us to be killed.

This was an interesting day for another reason. One guy had come to our unit right out of LBJ. He was a very gentle soul, so it was hard to understand what he had done to get himself jailed, but I never asked. Orders had come out to send him home, since he had been a civilian for a month. He, and apparently the record keepers, had thought that the stint in LBJ was bad time on his year in Nam. He went home a month after he should have been discharged. Lawyers would have had a lot of fun if he had been killed or injured.

Chapter 51

THE WORLD REVISITED

Jeanne went to visit relatives in Czechoslovakia. During this trip, she sent me a very nice letter. This was only a couple of years after the aborted Czechoslovakian freedom movement that Russian Troops stopped. Her letter to me was a correspondence addressed to APO San Francisco. I couldn't help but notice that the letter had been opened by some Communist, no doubt to make sure no information was going to the US Army. The letter was a month in transit. She had also finalized plans to meet me in Hawaii in a few months when I was scheduled for a week of R&R. I almost didn't make it.

I was due to meet Jeanne in Hawaii. This was only a few weeks after the trials of Hills 714 and 882. I knew that I wasn't in the best of condition, but maybe getting out of Nam would help. For the most part I had withdrawn into my own little world.

When I went down to Da Nang, I stopped at China Beach before going to the R&R center. While there I sat next to a group of Marines that were talking. One was whining that he was going on his third patrol in the last six months. It really irritated me so I rebuked him. He had put in a total of three weeks in the field during this time period. In all fairness, the combat Marines had

161

gone home and this guy was one of a group that protected the perimeter of the military base at Da Nang.

I went to the R&R center and traded in my Military Payment Certificates, or Funny Money, for real American dollars. Soon I was in civilian clothes. I felt a little funny in these clothes after being in grunt green for six months. I don't remember the China Beach area looking like anything seen on TV, but I remember relaxing on the beach for about an hour lost in deep thoughts.

However, I was able to snicker a little at the warning in Guam not to take photos of the B-52s, as if the Russians didn't know where every one was located. These same B-52s would later entertain me.

I had a couple of days to spend alone before Jeanne could make it to Oahu. I was having problems, and it wasn't just saying "over" while talking on the phone. Some firecrackers were set off. I almost hit the dirt. I walked near a bunch of guys in monk-like robes with ponytails on the top of their heads chanting Harry (sic) something. I took time to tell them they were the stupidest sight I had ever seen. A cop politely told me to move on. The biggest shock was that no one seemed to give a damn about what was going on over the other half of the ocean in Nam.

A few years before I didn't care, and now I realized how self-centered I had been as a civilian. This was what the grunts call the world, and it was a strange place. I was a full-blown grunt, and this place was no longer home. Jeanne showed up and we spent some time sightseeing, but things were no longer clicking. I was not the same lighthearted guy she knew in the fall of '69. In retrospect, I was devoid of all emotion. She sensed this and I had a feeling that it wouldn't work out. We drove around the island and found a nice deserted beach. Despite being with a wonderful girl and in Hawaii, I was mentally never able to get away from Nam.

When I got back to Nam and the company area, the guys were all there. We had a bunch of FNGs who were being trained. One day we were all marched down to the armorer to have our M16s checked out. I was slightly concerned because months before I had written Jeanne's name on the stock of my rifle with the sharp point of a bayonet. I was hoping this REMF wouldn't give me any grief because of the damaged stock. I also had a Colt bolt in an H&R rifle. I thought to hell with this guy, after all what could he do, send me to a combat unit in Nam?

The problem wasn't the stock or bolt. The barrel was worn out. In six months I had burned out the barrel of a brand new M16. I was given another 16 with some new replacement parts on it. Someone else would get to tote Jeanne in the future. The replacement Mike16 had no sentimentality connected with it and was never used in combat although I played around with it on the bunker line late one afternoon. It was fun just shooting a magazine on full auto and not toward an enemy.

Chapter 52

MILITARY GEAR

At one point, I broke the Geneva Convention Rules by having one of my brothers back in Iowa send me some Winchester 223 caliber hollow point varmint rounds. They were not good to feed through a magazine, but you could chamber one by hand. The first round that left your 16 would explode when hitting flesh making a hole a yard wide. I passed a few of the rounds around to some of the more discreet guys. I don't know if any ever hit the target, but they gave us a feeling of power when walking down the trail. Another innovation that I had sent from home was a 30 round M16 magazine. The military had not issued any yet, and it seemed like a must to me. Col. Shay saw me with it one time and asked if it was Army issue. I just smiled and nothing more was said. I eventually gave it to a point man when I left Recon. The gooks all had 30 round magazines. Why couldn't we?

Everyone knew a bayonet on a short light assault rifle was almost silly. Somewhere in Nam, some soldier or Marine might have killed an enemy with one, but I never heard of this happening. They weren't even good as a knife because the metal was too soft. Virtually all guys obtained a good hunting knife

164

somehow. I'm sure the Buck Knife Company was very profitable during the Vietnam War era. While I was being innovative with killer rounds and banana M16 magazines, another Strike Force guy went retro. He took a mill bastard file and made his bayonet into Captain Ahab's harpoon. It was a work of art and looked downright evil with its barbed spear point on front of a 16. I don't know what happened to it, but I never saw another one like it.

While on the firebases and in the jungle the grunts weren't bugged too much about how they wore their uniform. Some things were done to look tough. Some things were practical like putting your dog tags on bootlaces or wearing your insect repellant or LSA gun oil on the helmet strap. Other things were done to irritate the officers. All kinds of individualization took place. In the rear, a concerted effort was made to keep everyone in uniform by the book, but they were never completely successful. Helmet covers unlike fatigues were often decorated as they stayed with the grunt.

All kinds of pins and patches were available down at the Korean Laundry shops. Many were X-rated and others just anti-Army. My favorite patch said, "Participant South East Asia War Games," which are now valuable collector's items. One of our guys had a pin that had the letters FTA on it. It stood for "F**k the Army." He was told by the major to take it off. He told the major that it just meant "Flying to America" and the major told him to take it off anyway. One guy was told to take off his religious cross, braided from shoe stings. He refused to because it was a religious symbol. While in the rear, he was told to wear it inside his fatigue shirt.

Chapter 53

CHURCH AND BOOZE

We had Catholic Church services one day. This was only the second opportunity while in Nam. After the sorrows of the month before, attendance was very high. I'm sure many of the attendees were Baptists that wanted to reconnect as best they could with God. After all Protestant and Catholic Chaplains looked the same in green uniform. It was a different Battalion than a month before. Many of the wounded had returned from the hospitals. The Strike Force was combat hardened. The next time we got into a slugfest the other side would find this out. Recon had many new guys. We even got some lifers with a lot of stripes. Sabo worked hard to find some replacements with both rank and experience. Not that I cared but there was no chance of promotion.

The Army was depleting in numbers as the war wound down and there was a surplus of E-6 Sergeants. One day they told some of us Recon guys to go down and get issued helmets. Some of us were going to be decorated. They didn't want us Recon types to look different from the others so we also got brand new helmet covers. All of us veterans from Hills 714 and 882 looked ridiculous in new helmets and fatigues. Speeches

166

were made and then some of us were lined up and given medals. I stood next to L.T. Hill and Colonel Charles Shay, a former Marine, placed a cigar box full of things on my chest.

Author, L.T. James Thomas Hill, Col. Charles "Shamrock" Shay

The Purple Heart I received was manufactured in WWII when they expected hundreds of thousands of casualties in the invasion of the Japanese home islands. I felt very uncomfortable for some reason. Maybe it was because medals don't take the place of lost comrades. Maybe it was guilt for being alive.

It was soon over and most grunts threw away their new helmet covers and put on their old dirty marked up ones that labeled them as an old timer. Only FNGs had new helmet covers. This was the first time that I wore a helmet. The training was poor, but they kept emphasizing some old Army basics. Would grunts in Nam ever start to use fire and maneuver? Soon they did. Most of us combat hardened Recon guys were real jerks about the training and we didn't make any friends with the instructors.

One of our guys had come from the Big Red One with Gary Gear. He was a "woodsy" guy that everyone liked. He was in deep pain over Gary's loss and never got over it. He began hitting the sauce very hard and getting into trouble. He once took some shots to scare Top Childers after being assigned bunker duty.

Another time, while in disrepair, he got into an argument with a few black guys. A half an hour later, two black guys walked in the area and he took a few shots to scare them off. He thought they were coming to get him for the earlier confrontation. We quickly got him out of the way and a message was passed along as to what happened and that we would take care of the guy. No officers got involved as far as I know. There was no big racial incident this time. The grunts of the 2/502 were somewhat less racially divided than they had been before the battles of April and May. We watched Gary's friend 24 hours a day.

Most of the time, another friend shadowed him closely. I can still see him protesting his shadow. It looked as if the two were dancing as the friend kept him physically from going back into the bar. The sorrowing guy soon went home and I hope it turned out all right, but I doubt it. The VA should have taken him under their wings for consoling before releasing him from the military.

There were many other guys having problems. The lifer Sergeant, who I had given the on-the-job bunker elimination training to, and I were having a beer one evening during a stand down. The guy from months before who wanted to straighten me out came in totally inebriated and wanted to fight us both. He said everyone was calling him a faggot and he was tired of it. He wanted to strike out at something. He was obviously in much pain. We took a little time and talked to him and got him through his crisis. He didn't have a friend left in the world. He was going home soon and his few months as a hero were over. I had only sympathy for him by then.

Chapter 54

PREPARING FOR MORE BATTLE

One time, about six of us with a lot of combat experience were brought to a small rifle range for a little extra training. The officials wanted our input on a new shooting technique. Instead of using our rifle sights, or shooting from the hip, John Wayne style, we were ordered to perform the pointing method. It was a simple method that someone had started using in the field. You would place your left hand index finger on the forearm of the Mike16 and just point at the target. The 16 would go along with your finger as it pointed. When you pulled the trigger, the target you pointed at was hit. We all did very well using this method and really tore up silhouettes at 15 meters. This would not have worked on any rifle except an M16, which had virtually no recoil.

During my last few months in the field, I trained myself to walk with my finger on the forearm pointing ahead. I never received the opportunity to try this method in combat, and I don't even know if the military even started teaching this technique to all its combat soldiers.

A few days later, some of us Recon men were sent in to help with a new FSB that was being constructed. We linked up by the Major's beautiful bunker. My fellow Recondos were very upset that he had ordered them to build Taj Mahal-like dry mortar-proof quarters before the FSB perimeter was finished. One man proudly displayed a grenade that was stationed behind a foxhole right below the Major's bunker. Apparently a pact had been agreed upon that if the FSB was hit, the first grenade was to go into a hole in the fancy bunker. Talk is cheap as the saying goes, but I wondered if they really meant it.

An officer whose first priority was his personal convenience over the safety of his men was usually despised. That afternoon, at the last minute, Recon was told to patrol east of the FSB. We probably didn't go out as far as they wanted us to go. Frankly, we stopped just out of sight and crawled in some brush. If we had time to get prepared it would have been different. Patrolling at twilight was not good technique.

This was the only time this stunt was pulled, that I was aware of, in Recon, but it was common in Nam. The danger was that if no one patrolled, the enemy would soon be set up and knocking at the door. In jungle warfare, the aggressive units lost fewer men than the slackers.

Soon they loaded us up and sent us far north as fast as they could. I recognized the famous Khe Sanh site from the air. It was where the Marines had fought off thousands of NVA just a few years before. Now it was peaceful. Some Cobra gun ships had caught a whole North Vietnamese Company walking in close formation down a mountain trail and took them down. Several hundred of the enemy were killed in minutes. We were sent to guard a firebase while the local grunts were taking care of the few remaining NVA.

Right next to the helipad were all the captured weapons from the turkey shoot. There were hundreds of weapons in a very large pile. The pile was mostly made up of AK-47s and RPGs. There were about a dozen well-worn M16s. How was the enemy getting these weapons? Did they belong to dead Americans? Knowing how many had died in the long belch of a mini-gun was very sobering. I talked to a soldier standing by the weapons and he told me there were literally piles of bodies out there. I kept wondering when I would see my next combat.

Trouble was brewing up in this area. In early July, FSB Ripcord started taking 120mm mortar rounds. An epic siege, somewhat akin to the Khe Sanh battle, was just starting. Two Battalions had companies working around the area and they had been in almost continuous combat. Several companies were in trouble and the whole Strike Force BN was on standby to go in and help get them out. I doubt if many of us wanted to go into more battles like the ones we had experienced a few months before. All of the troops around FSB Ripcord and even Ripcord itself were soon evacuated. A decision had been made to pull back and let the "Dump Trucks" or B-52s do the work.

A couple of days after FSB Ripcord was abandoned, the whole 2/502 BN went up to an old Marine FSB named Maureen, a short distance southwest of FSB Ripcord and not too far north of our old trouble spot Hill 882. Our mission was to be as obvious as possible and draw the NVA our way. It took great effort to make a lot of noise and appear as if we were going to stay in the area. Shape charges were being used to blast rock for a giant heliport. A 106mm recoilless rifle was placed in the most obvious visible spot. The NVA had other plans and went after FSB O'Reily manned by the ARVNs. This was my first time actually helping build an FSB perimeter.

Fighting positions were made as new guys were being taught how to hide trip flares in the wire. They had to be taught because this was a different country. There were lots of open valleys with high pointed mountains where the wind blew continuously. Helmets and flack jackets were also mandatory at all times. The gooks had big 120 mortars and we were told to expect anything and everything. Expect the unexpected.

The possibility of a tank attack slowly became a reality. Rumors circulated that the 106mm recoilless rifle we had on Maureen was to fight off tanks. Our 90mm recoilless riflemen from E Company had anti-tank rounds. Another rumor floating around was that seven Americans froze in their bunkers on FSB Ripcord and never made it to the helicopters for evacuation. On FSB Maureen, you could see the mountain range that created the border with Laos. The trouble was that there were no Laotians on the other side of the mountains, only North Vietnamese.

View of Coc Muen from FSB Maureen

Another interesting thing on Maureen was the quad 50-caliber machine gun set up. I would often go over and watch the practice for enemy attacks. Quad 50s had been used effectively during the siege of Ripcord.

One time when they were practicing with it, they missed a grunt by a foot. I happened to be on the radio then and heard an array of colorful words. Maureen was never attacked. The NVA must have known it was the Strike Force on the hill. All day long the B-52s unloaded on Ripcord or areas near it. Lots of noise, light, and smoke entertained us. The second night there was a massive strike that hit all of Ripcord at once. The dark pointed silhouette of FSB Ripcord looked like a Christmas tree lit up with lights.

Chapter 55

DELIVERANCE

A re-supply helicopter came in and started unloading. L.T. Dan Johnston came over to me and said that Top and the "Old Man," now Captain Ciccolella, wanted to know if I could take a rear job in Company E. I asked with a little bravado if I could have five minutes to think it over. Those few minutes were used to get my stuff and say goodbye to a few guys from Recon. I walked back up and jumped on the chopper. They knew that I would take the job before I was even asked. Everyone knew that old timers were poor soldiers. I had bounced back a little since May but still was somewhat sullen. It was just a matter of time before fear came back as it did with many guys when they started to get close to the end of their tour or short.

Soon we were airborne on a clear late summer day. The whole A Shau valley could be seen from end to end. Laos and Dong Ap Bia, "Hamburger Hill," were easily seen to the northwest, Hills 714 and 882 to the southeast, and the scarred mountain where FSB Ripcord had been to the north. We went east toward the South China Sea and the long flat hill by Camp Eagle.

It was a beautiful storybook scene, but there was only one problem. I wasn't thinking about the lush tropics. I was thinking about how I was going to make it. I was going to make it home. I

173

was going home alive instead of in a body bag. This was actually a very common feeling that every soldier experienced when he returned from the other side of the line. I also felt a little guilt about leaving Recon, but it wasn't so bad. I hadn't bothered bonding with most of the FNGs. Only about three guys had been there longer than me. It was time to move on.

Top Childers was happy to have me there. Why me? I was a senior guy, but there were a few guys from E Company in Nam longer than me. Sergeant Major Sabalauski had me in the barbershop before I could even get to the company area. He bawled me out for taking a rear job instead of staying in the field. Fortunately, no one else faulted me since I had paid my dues in the bush. Soon they had me in nice solid green starched jungle fatigues instead of the Recon camouflage ones. My title was company clerk but my function was to be Top's assistant so he could stay in the office. There were many parts to the job including bartender and training NCO. A major part of the job was being mail clerk.

The next morning I was sent on an errand down the road to the local Korean laundry to pick up an officer's uniforms. They were a tough bunch that would look you sternly in the eye and say, "No ticky no laundry." I started walking back on the road looking as good as the day I did when I first reported nine months before. Almost immediately a whole convoy of grunts on the backs of deuce and a halves came down the road. One of them yelled at me in a very infantry voice, "REMF!" Soon others joined him and began taunting me. It hurt a little, but it's the price you pay for getting a rear job.

On the way back I ran into an arty guy that I had known many months before on FSB Rifle. He was the guy that owned the little puppy named Stud. I asked him about his dog. He told me that Stud had received all his vaccinations and papers in order to go back to the States but had been run over while chasing a bitch. I really didn't want to hear about any more deaths, even animal deaths. Death always came quick in Nam. The puppy had survived the night of February 11th when the sappers hit only to die in pursuit of doggie love. I heard later that Jo Jo the Battalion monkey wasn't allowed to go to the USA.

I was assigned a small cell in the personal storage and mail building. There was just enough room for a cot and a trunk. This of course was heaven compared to sleeping in the bush. I spent very little time there though. Most socializing took place in the company bar or the barracks. My bunk was in that building only to keep the mailroom and equipment room protected from theft. The previous occupant unwisely left all kinds of Polaroid pictures of his wife there when he went home. His poor wife probably would have killed him if she knew that her husband had been so careless with these very private photos. I did him the favor and got rid of the photos.

I always kept the room locked; yet it didn't matter. Twice the door was kicked in and both times my poncho liner was stolen. Grunts hated REMFs and instead of going to BN supply and trading in a worn out blanket, they would just steal a new one. Most of my real valuables were stored in the Company E headquarters that was manned 24 hours a day. As I was nearing the end of my tour, it became fashionable to disarm grunts when they came back from the field. One time at the beginning of a stand down, even before Sabo marched everyone to the barbershops, all ammo, grenades, trip flares, etc., were put on a pile right near the heliports.

View of 2/502 BN from heliports
Co. E directly behind stage
(Photo courtesy of John Roberts)

175

The logic was that Camp Eagle was secure and only one thing could happen if the troopers were fully armed. It may have had something to do with some ugly incidents that were starting to happen in Nam. Many officers and NCOs were starting to fear for their lives. Two rear echelon guys were sent up to the pile of armaments. They were supposed to sort everything out and put it away. Soon a trip flare went off and the pile was on fire. Instead of running away, the guys tried to put it out. They failed and the whole thing blew up killing both guys. Death was everywhere in Nam. REMFs were not immune.

Chapter 56

GUNS, SKULLS, AND NUDES

The Company E bar room was a plywood shack with a corrugated metal roof. There was a bar going all the way across the floor except for a small entry. The wall behind the bar had a mural of a naked lady. She looked kind of Vietnamese except for her breast size. Occasionally someone would ask in jest, "What's that?" Men were in the jungle so long that they forgot what a woman was.

Author and Charles Kinsey at Co. E Bar

177

The rest of the building was an open room with one large round table for playing cards. Poker was the most popular game and the stakes were high. The better players in the BN came over to Company E to play. One guy claimed he was sending a thousand dollars home every month. This was in a time when that was three months salary for a buck Sergeant including combat pay. It was not a place for low rollers. The goal was to keep the guys close to home and not go up on the hill to the Phoc Roc brigade club and get in fights.

Recondos at war, 1970
Jeff Yocum, Ron Hipp, Stan Hayes among others

A few months earlier I brought a nice Russian AK back from Hill 882. There was no chance of getting it home so it was donated to the clubhouse and mounted on the wall. Soon we would have another eerie memento.

We had a new guy nicknamed Bull come into Company E. He had been kicked out of Special Forces Training for being too aggressive. That is, he decked a training Sergeant. Bull had found a skull out in the jungle and slipped it into his pack. He polished it daily for a few weeks with his toothbrush until it started to look half way good. He proudly told me that he was going to mail it to President Nixon. I knew this wasn't smart because many packages were X-rayed before being sent out.

There was no way that it would be delivered to President Nixon without being opened first.

Several of us told him that it was a great idea, but we didn't want to see him sent to LBJ (Long Binh Jail). After a few minutes of very good advice, we convinced him that a better place to keep it would be the CO E bar. There was a ledge behind the bar that it fit on nicely. Later, it became a rite of passage for Recondos to drink beer out of the skull. I have photos to prove it. We now had a mural, an AK, and a skull. Plans were made to mount an RPG-2, but it never happened while I was there. A few years later there was a campaign by social leftists to mail cockroaches to President Nixon. Maybe they got the idea from Bull.

A few weeks earlier we had been forced into taking two more Kit Carson scouts. The new guys didn't fit in too well though. One of the two named Van left to visit his family for about a week. While he was gone, the second one was caught stealing a camera and was sent to the ARVNs where his pay would be much smaller and he wouldn't get by as easily as he had with us. Being an ex-Communist soldier could have made him a marked man. When Van came back from his leave, he started asking, "Where Vinh? Where Vinh?" Unfortunately Bull heard his pleas and came over. Bull told him to come over, and he led him up the hill to the CO E bar. He pointed to the newly placed skull and said, "There Vinh." Van went into a death roll, started wailing, and pulling out his hair. It took Bull about half an hour to explain that it was just a joke. We didn't kill people for stealing and then mount their skulls. We did something far worse. They were sent into the ARVN.

Chapter 57

BUNKER DUTY

One day Top Childers told me I had bunker line duty. When I reported to duty, I was put in charge of a bunker because of my rank and combat experience. All the others were REMFs or malingerers, which is the term the Army uses for guys that always have some reason to be in the rear. These guys had plans just to crash and do nothing all night.

I was a real hard ass and told them we would all pull two-hour watches with no "moving the watch dial" shenanigans. There was a lot of whining about how nothing ever happened on the bunker line. First watch started at 10:00 p.m. At about 9:00 p.m., a military jeep drove up to the bunker and asked if anyone wanted any dew, the local name for Cannabis. He even said, "It's already rolled by machine."

I told the guy, "Get the hell out of here!" This of course brought on some more whining from the crew. At least there were no death threats. I didn't want these guys stoned thinking how neat it was to see some guy creeping around in the bush. The bunker was damp and smelled of urine inside. It was dry weather so I crashed outside. About midnight some brass came by to see if anyone was awake. I hailed them with a loud yell,

"Halt, who goes there?" I did this in case the men inside were asleep.

I took over last watch but was extremely tired because I had been constantly checking on the crew. Soon I saw movement and it was real. They had given us a small hand held starlight scope. When I looked through it I saw the biggest rat of my whole life nosing around. A few years later I found out that it was called a bandicoot rat. Watching it scurry about kept me awake. Despite the fact that I hated bunker duty, I even volunteered one time.

Top Childers always liked to grab grunts back from the field and put them on bunker duty. They hated him because of this. It was why "Jonesy" shot up the office one time. He knew that a grunt with free time often created trouble at the Phoc Roc or worse.

Top did this on the day that Sabo gave his farewell party. This was going to be a big shindig with all kinds of treats never imagined in Nam. The grunt involved was kind of a troublemaker, but he was a combat grunt. I felt sorry for him because he was going back to the field the next day. I went to him and volunteered to take his place if he were to put on a clean uniform, go to Sabo's party, and try to behave a little. This was probably the most decent thing that I had done for another person in Nam.

I felt guilty for being a REMF and this combat guy had to go to the bunker. Luckily they put me up in the high tower with the big "Starlite" scope. Sabo's party was a big success. He had put in five of the past six years in Nam and was a highly decorated man. He was even known by Generals. He once decked a Battalion XO and no charges were filed because of his connections. He was an icon and later a legend in the Strike Force. The Sabalauski Air Assault School in Ft. Campbell is now named after him. Every man who went to our Battalion during his tenure remembered him. A character in the book *13th Valley* was really Sabo. Years later the author and Sabo met at a reunion. I guess Sabo didn't kill John for using his persona.

181

Chapter 58

CRAZY GRUNTS

One night, while sound asleep, loud explosions went off close to the hooch where I was sleeping. I grabbed my 16 and plopped on the floor outside my cell. I was waiting for someone to come through the door wearing sandals and carrying satchel charges. Soon I heard a 45 automatic going off and some English language taunting and threats. Funny thing was that the gooks weren't behind the attack. A gang of GI's came to kill Top Childers, yet had botched it. They threw grenades on the roof, but the round M-33s rolled off before exploding. REMFs didn't know how to cook them off. We did find a slight blood trail. I don't know if it was from Tops 45 or if his own frag hit one of them, but Top didn't tell me everything.

I found out later that a similar incident had happened while I was on R&R. It had been precipitated by the disgruntled medic that thought he was too good to go out in the field. A few weeks later the culprits were sent to LBJ. Top Childers was due to go home, and a new company Top Sergeant was arriving soon. I spent half a day filling the holes in company E's headquarters roof and walls with tar. A lot of guys came to inspect the damage.

It was hard getting the work done because some of them were undoubtedly the culprits involved.

Soon the whole Battalion came back from the field. Bar keeping for crazy grunts was a lot of work. The only thing that kept the guys out of the bar was a good movie or stage show. The second night they had a stage show with some real cute Korean girls. A new guy in recon started to act up and wanted to fight right down on the benches with a whole crew of guys from a line company. He had a lot of "Dutch Courage," but settled down. He was turning into a real feisty Recondo.

The next night a movie was shown and the guys were quiet for a change. I was put in charge of quarters and others relieved me from the duties of keeping the bar. The company office looked right over the movie seats. It was nice because I could watch the movie while watching the shop. One of Recon's medics came in with a few buddies. He was soaked with beer and full of bad memories of the twin Hills 714 and 882. I did something to antagonize him, and he tore all the photos of the chain of command off the wall from President Nixon down to our company commander. He then thrashed the room. I got him settled down and more importantly out the door. Another CO E soldier and I put everything back together. We knew that the next day Top Childers' replacement would arrive and we wanted the place to look nice.

Helping a Brother stay out of trouble

183

Early the next morning, a black Sergeant Major came into the CO E HQ and announced that he was going to be Top Childers replacement. Next he asked a question that almost floored me. He asked me what happened last night in the HQ. Apparently, he had been watching the movie and saw an interesting sideshow. I had this feeling that I would soon be back in Recon, but I gave him an honest response and simply told the truth. An old time grunt got out of control, but several of us settled him down. SM Wilson wanted to know if he needed any Army discipline. I told him I would talk to the guy and it wouldn't happen again. After that I shadowed my old friend when he was drinking. He never knew how close he came to being in trouble. What was the punishment for ripping the President's photo off the wall? In some societies, like Saddam's Iraq, it would have been torture and death.

The whole Strike Force, including Recon, soon went back north to another FSB near Ripcord named Barnett. Recon walked off the FSB about half a click when they were in contact. The point man was killed by small arms fire. SM Wilson told me that it was strongly suspected that he had forgotten to chamber a round. The slack man after expending all his M-79 thumper rounds crawled up and took the point man's M16 and discovered that it wouldn't fire. It worked fine after a round was put into the chamber. No one knew if it would have made a difference. He was hit in the head.

SM Wilson asked me if I knew our fallen point man. The dead man happened to be the guy that was ready to fight a whole company a few nights before. Since I knew the man, we made that long trip down to the morgue that evening. When the body bag was opened, I didn't recognize him. Even with a second look with a better light, he still didn't look like the guy I once knew. It was dark and they had to lift his head so I could get a lateral view before identification was finally made. There was no way that I was going to send the wrong body back to his family. This was another stressful time in my life. I was losing some of my hardcore mentality.

The next day I collected all of his gear and sent it to his family. The rules were to send everything back home to the soldier's family. There were no exceptions. Top unofficially said, "Take out any *Playboys* or anything that might upset the family." Recon had lost eight guys in 1970. He would end up the last man from Recon 2/502 killed in Vietnam. The war was starting to wind down and my time was getting short.

Russell "Barkie" Bahrke

A few days after "Barkie" died, a soldier from Bravo Company knocked out one bunker while on an assault and started to throw a second grenade into a second bunker. He was cut down by a burst from an AK. After he hit the ground, he reached out and pulled the live grenade under his body. He died instantly while saving the lives of his four comrades. Three guys from his squad told me the story a few days later. A few years later, he was given the Congressional Medal of Honor. I felt guilty because all these men were dying and I had left Recon right before some brutal combat.

The grunts from Bravo Company called this area "Come Back Ridge" because they cleaned out multiple NVA and a few days later went back to the same area and had to clean it out again. The 2/502 only had five KIA in this major campaign against the same units that had raised havoc by FSB Ripcord. Unfortunately I knew two of the five guys. This was a very one-sided battle fought by many veterans of Hills 714 and 882.

Chapter 59

DEATH OF ANOTHER FRIEND

Ever since the battles on Hill 882, I had been friends with
Alpha Company's RTO. We both sat down and compared stories
and even knew when the other was stretching it. He was always
unshakable, yet always had a grin. One story he told was how a
gook had a bead on him. He rolled to the left just as the bullets
missed him by inches and then as he rolled back bullets landed on
his other side. He explained that the combat was just like the
movies starring John Wayne. He admitted to me that he was
really scared sh*tless when this was going on.
    I was probably closer to him than any man in Nam
although we didn't see each other too often. I repaid his
friendship by always listening and of course giving him some
free beers out of the bar after I became rear echelon. There were
a few guys I knew from Recon, Alpha, and Bravo that had this
privilege. They had all paid their dues on the hills west of Hue.
    One day grunts from Alpha stopped by and told me that
my friend had been hit by a 51-caliber antiaircraft round while
flying in a chopper. This shook me up again since it had only
been a few days after I identified the last fallen Recondo. My
friend was said to be in critical condition and we all hoped for the

best, but he died several weeks later. He came from a large family in New Mexico and is still mourned.

After about a month of being an REMF I had the urge to go back out one more time in the field. I gave SM Wilson a BS story about some lost mail that needed investigating. He knew my true intentions, but allowed me to go. I went out on a Slick with the re-supply. Recon was set up in a nice pastoral spot. Some of the guys were sunbathing. They had taken off their very soiled camouflage fatigues and taken a dip in a stream.

The sun in late summer was great. These guys were smart to get a little tan and air their feet because the monsoons were due shortly. It was great to be back out with them even if for only a couple of hours. Some of the old timers I knew hashed over old times. It was also interesting to see how some of the new guys had progressed. There were only two guys that were in Recon from the time when I joined almost a year before. They all had extended their tour so they would be mustered right out of the Army instead of going to another post. Their faces looked tired and they were probably thinking of a nice warm cot at Ft. Campbell or elsewhere that could have been theirs.

Once a day I went down to BN to pick up the mail. My job was to sort it between E CO Headquarters, Recon, and the rest of E CO on the firebase. Sometimes Radar or 90mm recoilless rifles were on a different FSB. Every few days a new guy would join the company and an old one would go home so an updated list was posted on the back of my mail shack. The mail to Recon would only go out on re-supply day every three days unless they were on the firebase. Mail to the firebase would go out almost daily. Someone was always going back and forth on a chopper. Top Childers and later SM Wilson kept me informed on everyone's location. Incredibly, the system always seemed to work. The mailbags always seemed to be returned usually with some letters in them. One of the few perks of being in a combat zone was just writing the word 'free' where the stamp was supposed to go.

Chapter 60

SHADES OF LOVE

It didn't take long in the mailroom to find out which guys had girlfriends or wives writing to them. Sometimes the mailbag would have a very strong smell from all the perfume. Some guys received letters written to them everyday, but the letters wouldn't always come in chronological order. Sometimes a girl would write a letter simply addressed to "A Soldier" CO E 2/502.

There must have been an organization back in the states encouraging young women to write. These young ladies helped out when it was fashionable to dump guys in Nam or spit on them at airports on their return. Men without girlfriends always seemed to have buddies that lined them up with female pen pals. These gals were true American heroines.

A lot of skin magazines always arrived with the mail as well. Some were magazines like *Playboy* and others were just hardcore pornography. If a subscription expired and it was a *Playboy*, the label was taken off and it was sent to the soldiers. As stated earlier, many times I saw guys from Recon post centerfolds on trees for the gooks to find. Crazy times led to crazy things like that. One time I heard that an NVA soldier was killed and a centerfold was found on him. It reminded me of what a Priest once told us in grammar school. Never get caught dead with dirty pictures in your wallet.

Outright pornography was discarded unless it was someone's subscription. Every month, a wife-swapping club magazine would arrive for a guy that had returned to the world. One of the photos showed a middle-aged couple standing behind an American flag completely naked. The man was fat, bald, and bare-chested. The woman on the other hand looked like the wicked witch of the West including a nice mole on her nose. Her breasts were sagging badly and hanging over the top of the flag. It was a truly nauseating sight. I brought it to CO E HQ and we all had a good laugh. It was posted on the mailroom wall with the caption "This is what we're fighting for." It didn't last long before the Major asked to have it taken down.

Company E had a Vietnamese family that kept the company area clean. This included taking care of the latrines and shower house. They were a middle-aged couple with a shy, but attractive daughter in her teens. I felt sorry for their predicament of being removed from their farming village and being moved to a relocation camp. I would give them extra food and surplus things that were not needed by the company. After a few weeks in the rear, I noticed that the girl was always around me somehow. Soon it was very obvious that she had her eyes on me. Top noticed it too and told me one day very bluntly never to touch her. That took care of all temptations. Just as well. No good would have come of it. Maybe her parents put her up to it. She did have a nice smile though.

One of our guys from E CO had a woman writing to him about once a week. Instead of going back to the USA to be stationed, he went to Korea. We didn't know this at first and I just returned her letters. They kept coming with pleas written even on the outside to deliver the letters to him. I went to Top and he did some checking. We found out that he had a leave to go back to the States before he went to Korea. He apparently hadn't even bothered to look her up on leave. We kept forwarding her letters to Korea. The letters kept coming until I went home. It wasn't always the soldier that was the victim. I can

189

only guess that there was a pregnancy involved in this relationship.

Chapter 61

SELFISH SOLDIERS

In addition to the mail, sundries, and armaments, it was my job to get the laundry washed and sent out to the guys. It was simple enough since you just truck the laundry to the facility and a few days later go back to pick it up. The problem was getting enough uniforms. Socks were nonexistent for a while. It seemed that every time I went down to the BN supply, they were always out of this important commodity. Soon after getting my rear job, I noticed that a lot of REMFs were wearing camouflage fatigues. The rear was a terrible place full of malingerers and misfits. Many of them were too lazy to scratch an itch. Instead of having their laundry washed at the laundry shops, they would get their buddy in supply to give them new uniforms and socks.

Once these clothes were dirty, they threw them in the trash. I kept going through the trash in back of the BN hooches collecting all the socks and other washables. The loot would go in the CO E dirty laundry. These men only cared about themselves and didn't care that some guy out in the field had his feet rotting off because he didn't have extra socks. On time I saw a few REMFs with new official boonie hats. I knew that the only soldiers that hats were intended for were Recon. When I went to supply, I was told that they were all gone. Gone to REMFs that is. Not one hat had made it out to the field. This put me over the

191

line and I officially complained to the officer in charge of supplies, but it did no good. Recon men had to go down to the Korean laundry to buy a boonie hat. The guys in Co E always had enough socks only because I was a trash picker.

In order to keep my mind off the recent past, I drowned myself in work. Company E was soon the most organized in the area because the mailroom was perfect, and every guy's equipment was properly stored and even had a numbering system. All storage areas were inventoried and equipment put in its proper place. I found all kinds of neat things and returned them to the armorer. During those days, I kept myself busy and it was good therapy. A lot of time was spent getting the company area ready for the monsoon season. Plastic had to be put over the windows and small trenches dug around the tents. I was almost blinded by the plastic because it was covered with something acidic. Some company was probably sending their reject plastic to Nam.

Sabo was all Army and the first to get in any soldiers' face when he strayed from being perfect. He also was a soldier's best friend. He made a great effort to keep the troopers happy, even the ones like me who were really busy. He installed a basketball court in the open space by the movie theater. He knew that this would keep a lot of guys out of trouble.

Walter Sabalauski leaning on CP at FSB Rifle
This was untypical of the man.
(Photo courtesy of Charles Ciccolella)

The BN had a nice outdoor movie theater. I don't remember one movie that played there except "The Subject was Roses." Overall I didn't care for it too much except it was about a soldier returning home. I was just starting to fantasize about my own homecoming. We had a movie almost every night of a stand down. Almost none of them were about war. Who needed a war movie? The world was our stage.

We also had a lot of stage shows come in. Most were Asian bands that had cute girls who sung poorly. The favorite song was the one that ends with "We gotta get out of this place if it's the last thing we ever do." The song was predictable and I soon hated it. One night some guy was peeking in the dressing room and got caught. The stage manager then abruptly canceled the show. Several hundred grunts were livid, and I thought a riot was going to start. Nothing happened and a lot more beer was sold at the Company E bar that was the closest to the stage.

Before he entered the US Army during WWII, Sabo was a professional boxer with 30 Wins and 2 Losses. Soon we had a very professional ring in place and a call was put out for guys that wanted to box at the next stand down. Sabo, of course, was the referee. The first match was the heavyweight between two guys of different races. The black fighter was a well-known Sergeant in the BN who was in supreme physical condition. They found some overweight white guy that was a monster of a man from somewhere. The audience was divided along racial lines. I was expecting trouble, but it was a good clean fight as were most of the rest. As it turned out, Hispanics won most of the other fights. At one of the lower weights was another black-white match up. Most of the guys that boxed had some boxing experience, but the one boxer in this match up had only experience in street fighting. It was somewhat funny watching him until he was disqualified for illegal punches. If the Strike Force had stayed there a few more years, there probably would have been sports leagues and a swimming pool put in.

Chapter 62

HOT STUFF AND
COLD SHOWERS

Eating at the Mess Hall was a welcome break after months of eating out of a can. Once you took your malaria pill they would let you eat. All of it was American except for one item. They had a local Vietnamese hot pepper swimming in vinegar and salt on the tables. Sabo would always try and get the young cherry L.T.s to try one as a test of manhood. Most were too smart to try them. He would then gulp one down to impress them. Sabo had them brought in just for his enjoyment, both for taste and entertainment.

Some of the Vietnamese workers in the area would go into a meadow and come back with a salad of herbs and things. Only they knew from hundreds of years' experience which plants were edible. I never ate one Vietnamese meal during my whole tour.

There was always something going on. One time they gathered up some REMFs and sent them out on night patrol just outside the Camp Eagle perimeter. They were all given some of Recon's Camos. It was indeed a sorry looking outfit. One tall guy was about 100 pounds overweight and looked outright silly in a very small set of fatigues. Some of the grunts that were in the rear at the time started to taunt them. They marched out the gate at sundown and somehow managed not to get killed on a real combat patrol.

Company E was the smelliest outfit in the Strike Force. The enlisted men had only a primitive cold shower that worked when water was pored into a small drum. It was always out of water. During the hot part of the year, it barely sufficed. Most guys would go over to the Phu Bai bath houses if they wanted a hot shower, steam bath, or miscellaneous. You couldn't go in without being propositioned by prostitutes for several sexual acts.

When the Sea Bees down the road were leaving Viet Nam, lots of surplus equipment was passed around. One item was a pontoon boat that was being used as a shower. I convinced my officials to bring it down to our company area and mount it. At least we had a large supply of water when the company was in rear. I later found a heater, but never got it going before going home. I probably lowered the rate of VD by bringing in the shower. Johnnie and I had tried to get in the Sea Bee compound when they were leaving in order to five-finger an air-conditioner. The Shore Patrol wasn't phased by our BS pleas when we tried to drive in and get one. The Navy had its own wire perimeter to keep out the Army.

Chapter 63

MAJOR PAIN

Soon after Major Hamby got hit in combat in April the Strike Force got a new major as BN XO. He didn't work out too well and was replaced by another major. He was even worse, and the complaints came pouring in when we were told this one was staying. In the BN he should have been called Major Pain in the ass. To give a balanced view of his character, a few soldiers thought he was all right.

One time he put himself in for an award when a soldier was injured on FSB Maureen. The clerks in BN refused to type it up. He was somewhat under control until Sabo left. Then he had the rear as his little fiefdom. Many career officers can function very well stateside, but in war they were known as chicken sh*t to the WWII Veterans. In Nam, the mission was to kill the enemy and not play power games with the enlisted men. Major "Pain's" reputation was well entrenched long before I got to the rear. His first big hit was with the motor pool. Most men understood the reason for washing the jeeps at the end of the day, but he made them go underneath and scrape any road tar off the undercarriage with a putty knife at the end of every day. That was too much. The BN medics had to dust off all medicines every day with a feather brush. It was like this everywhere. Rumors started to go around that he was going to be fragged. It was taken seriously after the incident with Top Childers.

Soon he buddied up with his old foes at the motor pool and they guarded his hooch at night. We soon crossed paths. About 10:00 a.m., after the great August stand down, he came to the CO E area for a formal inspection. I had been working several hours getting the place cleaned up and doing my normal chores when he came into my hooch with Top Childers. Everything was in great shape except that I had forgotten to lock the door to my sleeping room. He nosed right on in and with his heavy Missouri-German accent started to lecture me about not making my bed. I took one second to pull the poncho liner up, close the door, and lock it. Then I told him to excuse me because I had things to do. Top Childers was not happy with me on the surface, but the major never had bed checks again.

The next time he was in the company I was in the middle of something and didn't bother to salute him. He didn't say anything to me, but Top got bawled out. The next time I saw him I saluted him left-handed. I never knew if he caught on to what I did. On the positive side, the Major did get a Chapel built in the BN area. He did this at a time when no new construction was supposed to take place. The chapel was finished just about the time I went home. The only other construction that took place was the building of an NCO club near the chapel. It had real whiskey for 50 cents a glass.

Eventually Major Pain liked me. He found out that there were a lot of rats (animal type) around the BN area. An edict was put out that all companies were to exterminate the rats. Traps were sent to all companies for this task. I just ignored the request. Top later came to me and said the major was hurt that no rats had been caught in the BN area. Apparently he had asked for a body count from all the companies. Top asked me if I could set a few traps to get the major off his back. There would even be an award for the guy who trapped the most rats.

I went to the Mess Hall and got some peanut butter and some strawberry jam. Within a few days I had quite a body count. The major was ecstatic and soon congratulated me. Apparently I had caught more rats than the rest of the BN ten-fold. The major asked for the secret to my success. About that time I realized that instead of being insolent I was playing his games. The rest of the companies probably were not that inept at rat catching, they were just still ignoring him. The Army never gave me that award.

Chapter 64

BOB CAIN REMEMBERED

On the next big stand down, right before the monsoons started and while SM Wilson listened to me complain about bar tending once too often, I got one last turn at bunker line duty. This was my third time, and I was starting to get into the routine. The greater part of the BN was watching a movie that night when the 122mm rockets started to come in. The NVA were aiming at the concentration of a couple hundred 2/502 grunts watching the flick. We watched the three rockets go over the bunker line and land in the Strike Force area. I had this terrible feeling in my gut that a lot of guys were hurt. Within an hour, a jeep came and the officer of the day told us that no one was hit. The news was wonderful to our ears.

The next morning when I returned to the BN area, I realized just how blessed we were. The rockets had passed within feet right over the guys at the show and must have missed the top of my hooch by inches. The rockets hit the road behind the mailroom and slightly damaged an electric pole. The blasts knocked the CO E sign off the mailroom and some shrapnel had hit the building. The sandbags had actually worked. A part of the rocket was lying on the ground a few feet from the back door of the mailroom. If the dinks had set their rocket sights one notch lower we would have made the stateside newspapers the next day.

I took this very personally because the enemy was never able to hurt me seriously in the field, and now they were trying to kill me in the rear. I was never that scared of flying bullets, but exploding things scared the hell out of me since the day Danny the dog died. The next day a trench was dug next to the seats by the movie theater for the guys to dive into if this happened again.

One day when I was real busy putting up sheet plastic over the windows in the company area before the monsoon season started, a soldier came into the barracks and asked if Bob Cain was around. This kind of threw me back, since it had been five months since Bob's untimely death on Hill 882. I took a little time to get the lump out of my throat, and I then told him that Bob was dead. He wanted to know more so I had to go through the entire day of May 20. He said he was a friend of Bob and he wondered why he hadn't written lately. I couldn't give him a lot of time, but did the best that I could. I was slightly spooked by the incident and told Top what had happened. Top told me he had a similar incident when someone came to find Bob a couple of months before.

The next month's 101st airborne association magazine had a remembrance from Bob's mother wanting to get in touch with guys that knew her son. It seemed like everyone wanted to know what happened. Thirty years later the guy that talked to Top found me. I will always wonder who came to talk to me about Bob. He might have known Bob was dead and just wanted to find out what happened. Memories of Bob's slow death in the jungle while his comrades surrounded him always stayed with me in the back of my mind. I always meant to write his mom, but living soldiers develop guilt and have great difficulty seeking out the family and friends of the KIA. I still have that magazine after all these years.

Chapter 65

MONSOON

The big thrust into the A Shau valley had been canceled earlier in the summer when FSB Ripcord came under siege. After the NVA had been punished around FSB Barnett it was decided that we would go into the valley right before the monsoons started. It was hoped that the weather would hold and hoped that the enemy would get the punishment of a lifetime in their own backyard. The entire 2/502 went into that mystical valley of death. One of the common statements in the 101st was a fractured version of the 23rd Psalm, "As I walk through the valley of death I will fear no evil cause I'm the meanest Son of a Bitch in the Valley."

We in the rear were worried that they would lose a lot of guys. The real worry should have been about the weather. It hit hard and fast. Re-supply day came and went with no choppers getting in. Now we were worried about getting them out. After about a week, the starving guys surrounded by a regiment of the enemy finally were re-supplied by parachute. I remembered a time in the so-called dry season when we missed a re-supply because of unrelenting fog and were starting to look for bamboo sprouts to eat. Running out of food is painful, but being in the jungle in Southeast Asia without medivac and ammo availability is downright dangerous. They finally got them out. The gamble paid off only in the sense that while the Strike Force was surrounded in the valley, the dump trucks (B-52's) killed hundreds of the enemy. We didn't know it, but the Army had bigger plans that would be put into effect in early 1971 when I was a civilian. It never quit raining before I went home.

Once the rains started there wasn't much to do in the rear. Doc Moreau was out of the field and was working at the BN medic shack. The two of us started hanging out and drinking. We had a lot of long talks about the happenings of the past year and plans for the future. He kept trying to lift up my spirits. I did the same for him. It didn't always work too well. We were both apprehensive about the future. Jobs, women, and the war were the main topics. Jeanne didn't write very often, and Doc would try to encourage me. We would yell at each other and still be friends. We did our best to help the farmers of the USA by alleviating the grain surplus. We never got into any serious trouble and it was good therapy. We both had reputations and were generally left alone.

While hanging around with Doc Moreau I got to know most of the other medics. I mentioned to them that my hip still hurt from a jump off a chopper eight months before. They told me to stop by the medical shack the next day to fill out a report so it would be on record. The hip healed itself in a few months after returning home, but my ears still ring to this day.

Chapter 66

MERCHANTS

Early one morning, Johnnie "The Cajun" Cadiere and I had to make a run to the Phu Bai PX to stock up on beer and soda for a stand down. We needed to get an early start so we left soon after daybreak. They were just opening the gate that went out of Camp Eagle when we got to it. A crew had just checked the road out for mines and we were the first out of the gate.

We hadn't traveled 100 yards when this very small child ran out in the middle of the road. I was riding shotgun so I reached for my 45 pistol just in case. The kid then started yelling, "Big sister! Big Sister! Two dollars! Two dollars!" Johnnie and I looked at each other and just laughed. We had seen this on several earlier runs in the middle of the day with an older pimp down by the road. The scene just broke us up. This was probably the youngest pimp in the world. There was a tent set up on a nearby ridge open for business. Our medics should have gone out there every day with their silver needles. There was a rumor going around about the black syph.

When you caught it you were sent to Thailand for special treatment and couldn't go home until you were cured. There was even a rumor that some guys never got to go home. When I

203

started working for a state laboratory a few months later, I found out that it was really penicillin resistant gonorrhea. When we were returning from this trip we were physically searched for illegal drugs at the gate. Johnnie and I also thought this was funny because the officer we had given a ride to on the way back was a known dew user. They didn't search officers.

PXs in Nam were not like those in the States. The Camp Eagle PX had almost nothing in it. Everything was usually sold out. The one thing they had plenty of was porno. Half the building, if not more, was full of it. Condoms were also found in large quantities. It was almost impossible to get routine supplies that soldiers needed. Things were even worse for grunts in the field. REMFs could go daily or have someone check on what was available and stock up for other men. A lot of stuff was resold in the black market.

About the only thing of value were the tailor shops in the area. You could get custom tailored clothing shipped from Hong Kong to Nam or home. A lot of guys had new civilian wardrobes made. Once in a while, the PX system would send a metal container with supplies out to a firebase for soldiers. One time when I was first in Nam, I bought an aerosol bottle of liquid cheese to put on some crackers. After two little squirts the can was empty. The PX employees had used the can for a while and then sold it.

Being a grunt was the lowest. These canister PXs helped the guys on the firebases, but rarely helped guys from the field. The Phu Bai PX was a little better. They were different than others because they wouldn't let you bring your weapons in. Johnnie and I had to chain and padlock our M16s or 45s to the Jeep before we went in. There was no way that we were going to drive the few miles between Camp Eagle and Phu Bai without weapons even in a safe area. A lot of guys bought time honored things like engraved Zippo lighters and other souvenirs at Phu Bai PX.

The US military forces in Vietnam didn't use either US currency or Republic of Vietnam Piasters. They used military payment certificates or MPC. This stopped an underdeveloped country from being flooded with a large payroll and kept US currency from churning illegal activities. The greatest fear of anyone dealing in the black market was a currency exchange. This happened once while I was in Nam.

Usually these people came to your location and took away your old MPC and gave you the same amount of new money. This happened all over the country the same day. There was a maximum that could be exchanged. If you had a wad of cash from illegal activities you had a sudden problem. You had to find other soldiers to exchange it for you. This always cost you one way or another. We had an exchange in late 1970 while on a stand down. I always wired my money home on a monthly basis so it was no problem to exchange a few bucks.

All of the Vietnamese that had accepted MPC in the villages for one service or another were stuck with worthless paper. One of the line companies had smuggled a working girl into the company during the stand down and she had been paid with MPC. I don't know if she worked out a deal to get her loot exchanged. The big time gambling winner had been sending his winnings home in aliquots so as not to draw attention.

There was also a maximum that could be wired. Another way to beat the system was to take your ill-gotten money and just buy merchandise at the PX or a PACEX catalog and send it home. The money exchanges didn't stop illegal activities, but did slow it down a little. A few days after the exchange a guy from Recon showed me a $75 wad of old MPC. He then asked if there was anyway that it could still be exchanged. I told him he had some expensive souvenirs in his hand. I wonder what the stuff is worth as collectibles today?

Chapter 67

EVERY MAN'S DECISIONS

My year in Nam was winding down, and I started to think of the future. I had a few informal chats with the BN enlistment NCO. There were many options the military offered me. One was to go to Ft. Sam Houston and go into Med Tech School like I had originally planned, but this seemed silly. I didn't know how the other medical trainees would have been able to tolerate a guy with a chest full of infantry hardware.

Another was to stay in infantry and apply for OCS. The thought of a formalized white glove school after being a grunt didn't seem inviting. I could have just re-upped and became a Staff Sergeant, but this would waste a good education. But the idea of signing up for something that would send me to Europe for a few years did appeal to me. I really don't know how I would have performed as a lifer.

After the first few years of Nam, I didn't have a great deal of ambition. Another thing was in the back of my mind. It was possible that Jeanne and I could get back together. The meeting in Hawaii had not been perfect — she saw a man that had just come out of a jungle of blood and scattered brains. The bad traumas experienced in the spring of the year were just starting to dim a little. I noticed in her letters a certain distance. One never really knows for sure how a relationship will turn out. These thoughts were spinning around a short timer's hardened skull. I was happy, but apprehensive now that I was short. The new guys were very jealous of me. I was now the old timer with Company E.

One day in the back of E CO, I ran into L.T. Hill. He had been in Alpha for a while and was even its Commander as an L.T. We were both a little sour about things. I believe he was nursing his second Purple Heart. I told him that there was no future in the Army and he should think about getting out. He was a little irritated with my comments. He definitely proved that I didn't know what I was talking about and went on to become a general. Almost no goodbyes were made. We mostly all went home and tried to forget Nam like it was a bad dream.

The monsoons had been going on for over a month, and I was only five weeks away from my DEROS date when I would not only leave Nam, but I would also leave active duty. It had almost been a year since I left the cold weather of Iowa and flew to the tropics. It seemed like a million years and at the same time only a few days. A few weeks before there had been rumors of men getting to go home early. I was now a cynical old Veteran and didn't pay much heed to such talk, but it wasn't a rumor. I was told to get ready to leave in a few days. I could have been ready to go in five to ten minutes.

More soldiers were being trained for Nam than there were slots so they were sending soldiers home early. There was a political aspect to this also. The homefront was happy to get their men home one month early unannounced. They brought a guy out of Recon to replace me. He followed me around for a couple of days learning all the tricks that took me three months to perfect. I went down to the armory to turn in my weapons. A lot had changed in the eleven months since I had been in Nam. It had become more like the stateside Army. I turned in my replacement M16. It had only been fired once just to test it since June.

What got my goat was the idiot REMF in the armory wanted me to turn in seventeen magazines. His records said that I had been given that many in Dec 1969. I had lost a few on Hills 714 and 882 and had compensated by carrying a lot more grenades. This guy wanted me to find some replacements or be charged for them. I told him we could go back out to the twin hills and probably find a few. The subject was dropped.

The usual papers were signed. I even had to take a formal oath that I wouldn't divulge anything about my tour in Nam. I was upset about this, but he need not have worried because very little was spoken for thirty years. Recon was out in the field. I still knew a few of the guys. I would have liked to see them one last time. Two months earlier, the last men went home who had been in Recon in December of 1969.

I had been the senior guy in E CO for two months. It was a position of status. In a few days I would be at the bottom of the heap again. Captain Jim Catlin wrote me a great letter of recommendation and SM Wilson gave me some Recondo memorabilia. The 101st Airborne gave me a Brave Eagle challenge coin. It meant more to me than the earlier awards. Now it's a valuable collector's item. I even have the original papers that came with it.

I was finally driven down to the airport in Phu Bai. It was raining like crazy. I got on a beat up old C131 cargo plane and we took off to Cam Rahn Bay. The plane had trouble getting off the runway because there was about 4 inches of water on it. My thoughts were "Don't crash and kill me on my way home." It was finally airborne and it slowly flew down to Cam Rahn. Just then I remembered that a full magazine of green tracers was still loaded on the AK-47 mounted on the company wall. I always wonder if they went through the roof when someone played with the trigger.

Chapter 68

ABUSE OF AUTHORITY

Not too much processing was needed when we got to Cam Rahn. About fifteen of my classmates from NCO school were there also. We had all had the same time schedule during our service. We graduated together, then went further to on-the-job training, were shipped to Nam at the same time, and now we were coming home together. We soon had a mini reunion going. The first topic of conversation that stunned me was the death of David Ogden who had died in combat in another BN of the 101. We had been together at Ft. Benning and Ft. Carson. We sat around and wondered who else got it.

Years later I found out that another soldier was KIA, while another was killed in non-hostile action. Lots of stories were exchanged. One guy killed a gook his first day in the field at high noon while eating lunch — a believable story since it was all too familiar. Another guy claimed that hot brass falling on him from an AK-47 burned him. This too was also all too familiar. Another former classmate had frozen in combat and was given a desk job. We were both somber and happy at the same time. After a while, my group and I had more processing to complete.

We turned in our MPC for real money. New stateside uniforms were issued and we went over to see the MPs.

Many grunts refer to MPs as military pricks instead of military police. I had been in the service almost two years and had never crossed paths with them other than the two Navy Shore Patrol guys at Camp Eagle. I had such encounters because I wasn't a perfect lil' angel. About fifty of us were led into a building that had a tavern-like partition at the end. We were told if we had any contraband to bring it forward and leave it on the bar — no questions asked; just lay it on the counter. Some neat stuff was turned in, mostly illegal weapons. Semi-automatic rifles that had been previously tagged were perfectly legal.

We were then told to pile our gear up in front of us. The MPs walked up and down looking at all of the gear. One of them stopped in front of me and asked, "What are these?" He was pointing to my prized machetes. I told him what they were, and he told me that they were untagged weapons and if I wanted to take them home they'd have to be tagged. I told him that the Phu Bai MPs had told me they didn't need to be tagged because they were tools. In an arrogant manner, he said that I could take them home, but I needed a permit the next day. This would of course mean going home a day late.

We argued a little and then I realized this jerk wanted my blades. They were made of pig iron so I easily broke them on the cement floor and handed them over. I got the meanest look from that dirty REMF. As we were leaving the area we could see two military pricks walking away with two duffle bags of loot. Almost all of it was non-lethal. These guys probably had a side business selling the stuff. A few of the guys started yelling at the MPs, calling them names, and even threatening them. They yelled back pointing at their 45s. They did have some kind of power holding a firearm. It was then I realized how naked I felt without one. I would have to get used to not having a firearm 24 hours a day.

PART THREE:

LEAVING VIETNAM

Chapter 69

THE GREAT FREEDOM BIRD

During those days, grunts often talked about the great freedom bird that would take them home. Unfortunately, some came home in boxes, and some never came home at all. Fortunately enough, I was of those to board the Freedom Bird alive. I was not overly happy. I had memories, both good and bad, that had occurred in the previous year. My reunion friends from the NCOC class of 6-69F traveled different ways leaving me alone with my thoughts.

It was a nice charter airline with attractive Northern European attendants. The only thing missing were cocktails. As soon as we were in the air, the young ladies changed into their miniskirts. Some of us had not seen many "round eye" women for a while so it took a while to readjust to the scenery. One of the attendants stooped over to serve a guy, and two rows of heads met in the aisle behind her.

The first leg of our journey was to a military base in Japan. There was a lot of yelling and cheering from the guys going home as the plane left the ground. One must remember that the majority of guys in Nam were not combatants. It was obvious because they were the loudest. I sat beside a guy who, like me,

212

had seen a lot of combat. The Silver Star and other awards told the story. We talked a little, but were very subdued. We soon developed a closeness that only combat grunts know. I had seen it stateside between combat guys and now I knew the feeling.

We had about an hour and a half to kill at Anderson Air Base in Japan. It was difficult to get into too much trouble. Many of us went into the Air Force base PX to get our uniforms in order. Brackets to hold the ribbons were the most popular item. I still think it was a shame of the military that with all the processing we had to go through no one helped get the ribbons in place so a soldier could go home properly. The whole situation was marginal at best.

We soon were in the air again. The trip home was much faster because the jets had westerly tailwinds. It was cool looking down at the budding industrial giant of Japan. Factories were everywhere, which looked totally different from Viet Nam. The last Asian landmark that I saw was Mount Fuji, a truly magnificent site. Interestingly, the first US landmark that I saw a few hours later was Mount Rainier. It looked similar, but better than Mount Fuji because it was home sweet home, good ol' American soil. God Bless America!

First view of USA, Mt. Rainier, 1970

It took about 24 hours to get processed at Ft. Lewis. Some of the returnees were giving men in Basic Training a true mouthful about what to expect in Nam. Since when were REMFs telling war stories? I thought this was quite odd at the time, but I quickly forgot about it because we were being led into a Mess Hall to eat a steak meal. It was Uncle Sam's way of saying thanks. What a guy would do for a steak meal. I wondered if anyone had volunteered for Nam just to get a steak. Hell, I had to admit it was good. I had passed up a chance for a steak when Sabo went home. Little things in life do help.

I had been awake for over two days and there was no time available for sleep. We stood in line for three hours just to be processed for fifteen minutes. I was given a quick physical. It was much too quick, as I found out a few years later, because those quacks marked my hearing as perfect even though I never was given a hearing test. Somewhere near the end we were given Army dress greens because it was too late in the year for Khaki.

When I went to get an overcoat they were out of my size. It was just my luck. I finally talked the QM into giving me one two sizes too large. It looked stupid, but I knew how cold Iowa Novembers were and, believe me, it was a smart decision. Years later I gave it to a 6' 9" tall ex-Marine who was an Episcopal Priest named Father Joe. He looked good in it.

We were given our discharge papers. I was not totally out because I was still a reservist for a little over four years. We went out to where a bus was waiting to drive us to Sea-Tac airport. One guy was so glad he stripped down and changed into some civilian clothing right there by the bus. I picked up his field jacket and the rest of his gear from the asphalt. It was a nice ride in the Cascades. The green Army buses didn't have chicken wire over the windows like they did in Nam.

Chapter 70

HIDDEN TRAUMAS
ON THE HOMEFRONT

I first noticed it at the airport. The glances, the looks, the basic indifference had become the norm. I never personally saw spitting or heard any negative comments at the airports, but I could tell the difference even from one year before. After the Mai Lai massacre and the Kent State incident, the widespread apathy about this war had taken its toll. A soldier was dirt, and a returning soldier from Nam was subsoil. Still, I was excited to be back.

I had hoped to call my parents and tell them I was on my way home a month early, but the first flight east was to Denver. I probably stunk because I didn't have a chance to bath since Nam. Despite not having any sleep for two days, I never fell asleep. My voice was probably the best sound that a mother, who lost two brothers in a previous war, ever heard. I told my mom that I would be in Eppley Airport in Omaha in a couple of hours.

When I bought my ticket in Denver, I asked the girl who was selling tickets if the plane was almost full. In the past they always looked around to see if supervisors were in earshot before giving an honest assessment. If it had plenty of empty seats, I usually took military standby, but she said that the plane was

215

almost full. When I got on board the plane was almost empty. I was either losing my boyish charm or the airline girls were not giving breaks to soldiers anymore.

Mom and dad met me at the airport. It was cold and a few flurries were falling. We only talked a little on the way home. The family dog, Muttly, which looked like a Vietnamese yellow dog, gave me the big sniff over. He must have thought me a goner who had returned from the dead. When I got home the uniform came off. At first I was going to wear it to Church that Sunday, but I decided not to. After a home cooked meal, I retired to the couch for a short nap. The "short nap" lasted about thirty hours.

The grunts in Nam used to say how many days they had left in Nam plus one wake up day. I woke up reaching for my nonexistent rifle. Some strange guy was talking to me while I was half asleep and I asked him what the hell he wanted. As it turned out, he was my sister's boyfriend, Ray. I'm sure that I didn't make a good impression, but maybe that's what people expected from a Vietnam Vet in the early '70s. I had to readjust to society and become civil again. Death must have followed me home, since Max the family cat died a day later. To make matters worse, the reality of life hit me. I had no job, and my soon to be ex-girlfriend in Minnesota hadn't written much lately. The next day I planned to go to Carroll to shop for some clothes.

That week a terrible tragedy happened in Carroll. A young Vietnam Veteran a few years behind me in high school killed a guy at a party. The party was for a guy that was going into the military. Some of his friends started to tease him about his courage. He was asked if he was afraid to go to war and if he was afraid to die. The Vietnam Vet had been home a few months and was a troubled man that had seen a lot of action. He retrieved a shotgun and held it to the other guy's head and asked him if he was afraid to die. Unfortunately, the kid gave the wrong response and the shotgun somehow went off. It was the talk of the area. I could not have picked a worse time to come home. No one said a word to me about it. That's what bothered me. I felt like a marked man.

The next day we went to Carroll. As I was trying on a winter dress coat at Eddie Quinn clothier, a friend of the victim came in and asked if there was any way that he could buy a suit for the funeral. He was a fine young man, but couldn't afford one. Eddie let him rent a suit for less than the price of a dry cleaning bill. It was one of the most decent things I ever saw one human do for another. Good things still existed in this twisted world that I had become accustomed to.

About an hour later, I was buying a pair of shoes across the street and I pulled out my 101st Airborne waterproof jungle wallet. An older man near by asked me where I got the wallet. He said that he wore that patch in WWII and knew a lot of guys that had died wearing it. I told him that was still true, and that nothing had changed. No more had to be said. I discovered the Brotherhood between all guys that were once Screaming Eagles.

About a week later, I stopped for a while at a party in Glidden. I wasn't in the right mood and left. On the way out, I ran into Russell Sparks, the younger brother of Don Sparks. We talked for a few minutes. In the conversation I told him that I hoped Don was all right, but I didn't have much hope. It was probably not the thing to say to a family member, but I had no optimism left in me. Nam to me was a place of death, not hope. At that time no one knew that Don had written two letters around the same time that I was hitting the worst of it in the spring of 1970. I once had feelings of being close to him when I was down by Bach Ma, but all those feelings of hope were dashed out on the twin hills.

A week later some guys threw a party in my honor. They probably just needed an excuse to have any sort of party. Shortly after the party started, I saw something that surprised me. This guy took a bottle of beer and ripped the lid off. I just thought he had a strong grip. I shortly found out that the twist off beer cap had been marketed during my year in Nam. There were many other small things that had changed in the past two years during my absence.

During the party, several guys spent what seemed like an eternity bragging about their high school football exploits. I had a few too many beers and finally said in a belligerent voice,

"Who in the hell did you kill!?!!?" Needless to say, I ruined the evening's fun. I was actually surprised that anyone wanted to party with a Vietnam Vet in the Carroll area since I wasn't in the best condition. Going back to the world and adjusting was much harder than going to Nam.

Chapter 71

BURNING VIETNAM

I was home about three weeks before I went to visit Jeanne in Minneapolis. I really didn't want to go because I knew that it was going to end. I was not the person she knew a year ago, and things had not gone well in Hawaii. The weekend was very nice until Sunday afternoon when she told me that she was already dating someone else. On the drive back, I realized just how devoid of basic emotion I was. It actually hurt me more when I lost "Jeanne the rifle" back in June.

Later that month I met another old girlfriend. She was a nice person, but I was somewhere else in body, mind, and most importantly soul. I saw her a few more times over the next few months, but I never came out of my depression during this period. I thought of visiting my friend at the Pi Phi house in Ames. I had not written for two years and never got the nerve to visit. I was young, alone, and had no idea what to do with my future.

The work prospects were not very good in Iowa at the time. I applied for a second semester teaching position and was politely told that 263 people had applied. Most were probably more qualified than me anyway. Graduate school was a possibility, but I had no academic ambition left. The same professor who talked with me two years before about getting into graduate school wasn't even interested in me now. I finally got a position in the State Hygienic Laboratory in Iowa City. I settled into the grind of work without much enthusiasm. This was a major career change, and I didn't even know it.

One of the part-time girls working at the lab had a husband in Nam and was worried about him. I tried to encourage her, but it didn't work. I kept telling her that if I made it, he could make it. The months started to roll on and I slowly got better. Another girl told me that I was brainwashed by the Army. Students didn't give Veterans any credit for being rational people. Frankly, most students at the University of Iowa were brainwashed in those days.

One night my two roommates and I went to Joe's Place in Iowa City. All of a sudden I was face to face with Hugh Perry. About a year earlier I had put him on a dustoff with five holes in him and sent him home. He was now in law school at the University of Iowa. We talked for about twenty minutes and I updated him on some of the tragedies that happened the month after he was hit. We never looked each other up again in Iowa City. We were both coping and wanted to forget. This was the last time I talked with anyone in great detail about Nam for thirty years.

Chapter 72

THE LEFT WING ENEMY

In the spring of 1970 while I was in Nam, the University of Iowa sent students home without having to take final tests after the students rioted. They were hoping to get out of finals again in 1971. This time I was there as the students began to gather on the grounds of the old Capitol. Soon there was a riot and they ran across the street throwing stones and bricks through the windows of the bookstore. It was a symbol of capitalism to them so it had to be destroyed. I stood there watching and musing on what a platoon of grunts from Nam would do if they saw this shame on the University.

A cop interrupted my thoughts when he came over to order me out of the area. All I was doing was standing across the street from the riot. I firmly believe that anti-Vietnam war feeling had very little to do with the riots that plagued Iowa City for those few weeks.

During the next few days, more and more Iowa State troopers moved into town. The students had to take their finals after all. The leftist establishment had taken over the vocal positions in both the faculty and student body. For years I was ashamed to admit that I worked for this institution. Before, during, and after going to Nam, I was somewhat apolitical about the politics of the Vietnam War. What bothered me about the scene on campus was the blatant anti-Americanism. The student newspaper was even worse. AP releases were changed to read--- *Capitalist forces fought a pitched battle with the Defenders of the People yesterday.* It was the same old leftist drivel.

In late spring, I answered a want ad for two bookcases. When I went to see the merchandise, the seller looked very familiar. He was Don Smith, a famous campus radical at Iowa State three years earlier. He was a very soft-spoken man who was working to get a PhD in History. I knew who he was and he figured out that I was back from Nam. We had a very civil conversation about the military. His main point in the conversation was that the ROTC had to go from the University of Iowa. My reply was that joining is a personal decision. No one is forced to join ROTC. We left each other without changing the mind of the other.

The left in those days didn't really want freedom. They wanted to dictate the rules. Don was a good example of how the campus radical perceived the struggle. One time, the local radicals marched down the street and were met by a counter-demonstration of local townspeople. The people in the counter-demonstration were not there because they loved the Vietnam War; they were there because they were sick of campus radicals and anti-Americanism. The struggle went on.

Shortly after starting to work at the Lab in Iowa City, I had a guy working for me who had to go to court for charges placed against him two years earlier in a riot in downtown Iowa City. John acted the part of the campus radical, but he was actually a very straight man. He told me how he was at a demonstration in downtown Iowa City in 1970 and a confrontation started far up ahead of him. The police department then charged the crowd, and he was knocked down by the retreating crowd and twisted an ankle. Despite telling a cop that he was injured and unable to do anything more than watch the demonstration, the cop started to beat him. He had to beg for his life in order for the cop to stop; then he was arrested.

222

At the hearing, John told the judge his story from two years before and all charges were dropped. He even got his bail money back at a time when he needed it. An even uglier scene happened in the spring when I was in Iowa City. Problems started downtown and the cops ordered the bars to close. Some innocent people, including women, who left the bars, were beaten before they could get out of the area. There are two sides to every story, but there is always right and wrong.

Chapter 73

SECOND CHANCES

I shared an apartment with two guys in the spring of 1971. They were exactly like I was three years before. The prospect of military service bothered them, like it did me in 1968, because it interfered with their lives and careers. One of them didn't think he would pass the physical, but the other was very athletic. One day in a candid moment, I told him the surest way to avoid combat in Nam would be to join the Marines for two years. The last of their combat units had left Nam. It would be better than waiting around for months to get drafted and putting in two years anyway. I don't know if he took my advice. Actually if he was drafted, he would not have seen combat since the Army was just about done fighting by the fall of 1971.

Another thing going on in those days was the birthday lottery. The good thing about it was that a person could plan his immediate future. I laughed about the lottery because my birth certificate was off by a day. I had two dates that could have been used. The lottery really didn't mean too much because there weren't many men being drafted. The American phase of the war was rapidly winding down.

Soon the word was released that two letters written by Don Sparks were found on a dead NVA political officer. This was proof that he was alive in the spring of 1970 months after his disappearance. The closeness that I felt to him down by Bach Ma had some merit. I had given him up for dead based upon my general feeling that no good ever came out of Nam, but there was hope. There was a chance that Don had made it. To this day I have some hope, even though it is very unlikely anyone will ever see him again. I denied him once and will never do it again.

I had figuratively died in Viet Nam and was depressed for the first eight months back. Part of it was Nam and part was the terrible pain of adjusting to civilian life. I had lots of guilt because I was alive and others died or were seriously wounded. In retrospect I had seen too much death. Most Vietnam Veterans received no consoling when they came back, though it would have helped. Soon things seemed better, and I started to get back on track. A good part of the home brew therapy was to bury Nam, and I did this very well. It was now only a bad nightmare that didn't seem real. Socializing started to happen and enjoying life slowly came back. I started to open up and people responded. I started dating and developing a circle of friends. I would never be totally the same as I was before Nam, but the future was looking better. I was twenty-four, I had a job, and I was alive.

One night in early September, I had a date with a girl who truly bored and depressed me. I told myself to find another date for the weekend. Opportunity struck again and the next day a young student who worked in the lab office many blocks away called about a lab form problem. I had met her months before, but had not taken an interest in her because of my depressed condition. She went to Europe that summer and had just returned. I asked her out after the business part of the call was over. I don't know why. Maybe the subconscious had been tuned into the pretty young girl with the long blonde hair all spring. We were married the following April.

Soon I felt like I did before the Army — I was somewhat uncaring about what was going on over there. The leftist establishment started to negatively stereotype Vietnam Vets, and it was best just to forget it all. I vaguely noticed the great NVA offensive of 1972 and the bombing campaign that finally brought the American part of the conflict to an end. There were always reminders.

One day I read in the local paper how Jack Nelson had set the record for walking across Death Valley. Another time the national news mentioned the two guys taken from our company in NCO school in 1969 to be questioned about Mai Lai. They told all they knew and charges were dropped. For a second my bride thought that I had been there when I commented on them. About a month before the Vietnam peace treaty was signed, another guy who I knew became a POW. William Wallace Wilson had been an Adelante Fraternity brother of mine at Iowa State. He was only held captive for one month after evading his captors for about the same length of time.

The only thing that got my interest in this was that Don and Bill were coming home soon. I was troubled when Don wasn't on the list of returnees, but I figured he was incarcerated down south someplace and missed the list of the guys returning from the north. Watching the guys get off the plane tore my guts out. When Don didn't get off the plane, my door on Nam was almost sealed. It was over for me. Even the fall of the Republic of Viet Nam in 1975 meant only a little to me.

I felt inside that the 2/502 guys of 1970 could have turned back the whole hoard. Some of the great liberals in Iowa City jumped with glee when Saigon fell. One guy went so far as to rub it in my face. What bothered me most was hearing that FSB Bastogne had fallen and my old friends of the 1st ARVN Division the elite of their Army had turned tail and ran without giving a fight. Freedom belonged to those willing to fight for it. All of this led to a situation where millions fled or were killed in South East Asia. The leftist establishment didn't say a negative word about all of this.

One thing that irked me a lot when working for the Hygienic Laboratory were trips to the morgue. They thought that because I was a Vet and a male I was the best person to go over and pick up autopsy specimens. It was not a pleasant place because it always brought back thoughts of mangled bodies from years before. Even processing specimens was sometimes difficult. I had seen too many bodies blown apart and working with little chunks of brain was not the high point of my work. One time they had a guy lying totally naked on a dolly full of shotgun pellets. They should have sent one of the girls.

Chapter 74

FACING THE GHOSTS

In 1982, JoAnn, our three sons, and I were living in Helena, Montana. A guy there found out that I was a combat Veteran of Nam and asked me if I wanted to go down to the dedication of the Vietnam memorial wall in D.C. I had no interest and made excuses. I knew Nam had affected me for the previous twelve years, but thought it was best to keep it buried since I was doing all right. I was enjoying life and was much better off than my eight dead Recon Brothers and Vinh. I knew what was bottled up. I did have recurring nightmares. The most common one was the one of being alone in a jungle full of NVA without my rifle.

One time while hunting for elk in the mountains northwest of Helena, MT by Canyon Creek, I came out of the woods into a clear cut. Some bullets came flying by too close. I wasn't a bit frightened. In fact the sound of zinging bullets felt good. L.T. Ciccolella's old comments were right. Nothing you would ever do the rest of your life would come close to the adrenalin rush you get in combat. I felt the rush again like it was an old friend. Common sense made me duck into the safety of the woods. Some guys had been sighting in their rifles. The dreams came back for a while.

My family suffered a little. This time it was the one about the jammed rifle when the gooks were coming up the hill on 714. Twice in Massachusetts I've been down range of shotgun slugs. Neither time did I flinch, not even in the slightest. I just stood there waiting for deer to run by. My subconscious doesn't believe any bullet can hit me. I was down range of probably a thousand rounds in Nam. Some Veteran friends have told me that there may not be a bullet with my name on it. Then they told me that some bullets say, "To whom it may concern or occupant." They had been hit in Nam. The thing that scared me the most in Nam were the explosives that tore bodies apart and emptied skulls out on the ground.

In the 1980s JoAnn's sister moved back to the D.C. area. During a visit we went sightseeing in the Capital area. She led us to the Vietnam Memorial Wall, which wasn't planned. I started to look up some names and started choking up. I got us all out of there quickly. The memory surge was too great. I had to quickly bury Nam and drive on. I have been to the wall twice since then, but I need some courage in order to make my final reconciliation with all the dead that I knew.

In the mid 1980s, I contacted the VA about the ringing in my ears that had been going on since May of 1970. The ringing had slowly become worse through the years. Sometimes I wound up having momentary total deafness in one ear. The VA checked my ears and said that I had high frequency hearing loss. They also told me that temporary deafness like I described doesn't happen. The DAV helped me file a claim, but it was turned down because the claim was turned in over a year after being discharged and my records said that my hearing was fine in November 1970. I know that I never had my hearing tested at Ft. Lewis. I thought this refusal was slightly absurd since I have Bronze Star records that describe being very close multiple times to grenade explosions. The good that came out of this is that I got some good counseling about protecting what I have left. I wear earplugs when sawing, mowing, and most of all I avoid loud noises. Tinnitus is something that cannot be quantitated or cured. Many a night, I wake up and listen to the loud ringing in my ears. The loud, continual ringing will be with me until I die.

In the early '90s, I was waiting for JoAnn to come down from an airport exit at Bradley Field in Hartford, CT. Out of nowhere this Asian guy came right by me with a pith helmet and a uniform. My mind saw me spring at him, put a chokehold on, and break his neck with my knuckles. The adrenalin rush was off the scale. I was like Dr. Pavlov's dog still conditioned to kill anyone who looked like an NVA soldier. What stopped me was the slight brown tinge to his uniform. It was a frightening mental trick that could have ruined my life.

Needless to say the dreams returned and hung on for a long time. The horror of being within feet and sometimes inches of armed enemies had been etched very deep in my mind. The family had to put up with me again. That fall I sold my NVA helmet and other uniform souvenirs from Nam at a gun show in Springfield, MA. I had tried to give them to an American Legion Post in Iowa City and later one in Helena, MT. Neither Post was interested. Some guy in New Hampshire has Vinh's uniform now. There is a good market for these things that I was ashamed to keep. I was hoping that these items, which reminded me of Nam, would take the bad dreams away.

The dreams became more frequent. The final blowout was the result of these things bouncing around inside my head for thirty years. Over the next year and a half, I confronted every demon. I did this by addressing exactly what happened in 1970. I identified what the problem was. The trauma of combat had been too great for me to bear. Withholding my emotions was the wrong thing to do. I started talking with other Veterans and found that I was not alone. Most of us came back home to an indifferent society and buried our past. We had misplaced a lot of the guilt. I found out that this PTSD could be beat if I had the willpower.

I am now an obnoxiously happy person. I spent a lot of time talking with Veterans of all conflicts. I may have even stopped one guy from killing himself like one of my old Captains from Nam did. We shared a bond that can't be put into words. A lot of my correspondence ended with "Your Brother in war and peace." I am slightly jealous of Veterans from the Gulf wars. They were treated much better because Americans realized that attacking the soldiers of an unpopular war is very unfair. The days are over when a coward will ask if you killed any babies over there. This was asked of me, just like Bob Cain, one time about a year after getting home. Bob Cain told us the truth about the homefront before he died. It won't happen to any future Veterans. Many of us Nam guys will make sure of that.

Chapter 75

TRUTH AND FREEDOM TRIUMPHS

I have met and corresponded with many people from the Nam days. Most of these encounters have been beneficial for all of us. Some didn't respond or didn't want to go any further than saying, "Good to hear from you," but I respect that. A few years ago I was just like them.

I hope to put a reunion together of all Recondos from 1965-1971. This is a major undertaking. Some have passed on, and it has been many years. It is hard to imagine guys like Kelly Torres who lasted three tours in Nam and then ended up dying in an automobile accident. One death was a shocker. I ran into several Internet inquiries of people looking for Bull. I visited a Strike Force guy in Bull's old home area and called everyone with his last name. One guy said that a cousin had lost a son by that name, but didn't know the circumstances. A couple of months later, I found that Bull had been murdered in 1972. In 1982, a group of guys made a list of every guy killed in action in the Battalion. Ft. Campbell has a monument for them.

People still remembered and cared for them. Bull should be on the list even though he died a year after his return. Camaraderie ran deep. An Ex-Recondo met Bull's sister and

232

flowers were put on his grave. I went to Eisenhower Park in Long Island to see Bob Cain's name placed on a memorial, and I found his name on a plaque at the local VFW. Several guys in Ohio have been in communication with Gary Gears' wife. Recondos from 1967 had a small reunion in Florida and met the mother and sister of a fallen Brother. Four guys wounded on May 20th got together in Ohio. There was an informal network out there that helped out. We later got together to say goodbye to Ben Slider when he was dying of cancer. Mike Ackerman, Fenton Flying, John Underhill and Randall Sherman are also gone.

Life and death went on for a while after I left Nam. About the time that my shoes touched the soil of the USA, Delta Company lost two guys. The gooks responsible ran right into Recon and were dispatched. There were some wounds in the Recon Platoon, but no one died. A few months later, Recon was working with a dog. The dog was let free to find the dinks. He found them, but was shot. They last saw the dog being thrown on a raft by some enemy soldiers. They probably were going to collect the bounty on it and also have a nice red meat supper. Dogs and Recon never worked together well. Later several Recondos were seriously injured when rotors hit their legs from a Huey that was shot down. The last combat by Recon was in July of '71 when five guys in a "safe" area went on a water run to fill up canteens. They met up with a lone NVA soldier that was surprised to meet any Americans. A few months later they were taken out of the field to avoid the health hazards of the monsoon season. What had started in July of 1965 was over by January 1972.

I hope to write a history of the Recon Platoon and maybe one on Sergeant Major Sabalauski. There are many good and tragic stories to be told. Another undertaking that has crossed my mind is writing a major article on the battles west of Hue on Hills 714 and 882. The public now respects the Viet Veteran for the most part, but doesn't understand much of what it was like. The number of dead in the Vietnam War was dwarfed by the casualty figures for previous wars, but the pain suffered by the families was far greater because of the feeling that they had died in vain.

The attacks on Viet Vets defamed the dead as well as the survivors. Even today I can't explain why guys I knew fought like tigers when no one cared back home. It wasn't heroism, or the seeking of glory; it was because Brother Recondos were bleeding in the kill zone. They would have done the same for me.

The battles fought west of Hue are still not over for some. They will probably go on until all of us who were there are gone. We fought a good fight then and won. Hopefully we will win the next battles also.

For me, the lesson of Vietnam is that freedom is constantly under attack from within and from without. The enemies within are the most dangerous for they sway the ignorant by misrepresentation of our purposes and intents, and thus they weaken our resolve to defeat the enemies without.

I am proud to have served in Vietnam and to have been a part of the victory of the soul, which the war ultimately represented to me.

Sources of Information
other than my own memory

History of the 2/502 Infantry 1970 "unofficial"
Official records 2/502 Infantry April and May 1970
The 13th Valley by John Del Vecchio
Stolen Valor by B.G. Burkett and Glenna Whitley
Thomas Boyce
Bob Childers
Clarence Cogdell
Charles Ciccolella
Terry Downey
Dave Hepburn
Lloyd Hume
Charles Kinsey
Mike Lucky
Tony Maab
Ron Meese
Tony Nappi
John Roberts
Louis Sanchez

Author and Charles Kinsey, 2001 Reunion

"Okie" Herschell Martin, Bernard Slider,
Gordon "Bob" Childers, and David Hepburn
2002 Reunion

Author, Charles Ciccolella, Thomas Boyce
Reunion, Veteran's Day 2002

Dave Hepburn, Herschell Martin, Bernard Slider,
Gordon "Bob" Childers, and author
2003 Reunion, just before Ben passed away

Sgt. James Brinker gets Bronze Star

U.S. ARMY, VIETNAM (AHTNC) Sept. 18--Army Sergeant James P. Brinker, 23, son of Mr. and Mrs. Joseph P. Brinker, Route 2, Glidden, Iowa, recently received the Bronze Star Medal and Purple Heart Medal in Vietnam.

He received the award for distinguishing himself by valorous actions. The Bronze Star Medal, adopted in 1944, recognizes acts of heroism performed in ground combat against an armed hostile force.

Sgt. Brinker received the award while assigned as a clerk in Company E, 2D Battalion, 502D Infantry, 101ST Airborne Division (Airmobile).

He entered the Army in January 1969 and received basic training at Ft. Polk, La.

He is a 1964 graduate of Glidden-Ralston High School, Glidden, and received his B.S. degree in 1968 from Iowa State University, Ames.

Notice how they called author a clerk—
many a pencil was thrown at the NVA

238

THE UNITED STATES OF AMERICA

TO ALL WHO SHALL SEE THESE PRESENTS, GREETING:

THIS IS TO CERTIFY THAT
THE PRESIDENT OF THE UNITED STATES OF AMERICA
AUTHORIZED BY EXECUTIVE ORDER, FEBRUARY 4, 1944
HAS AWARDED

THE BRONZE STAR MEDAL

TO

SERGEANT JAMES P. BRINKER, ███████████, UNITED STATES ARMY

FOR

HEROISM IN GROUND COMBAT

IN THE REPUBLIC OF VIETNAM ON 27 APRIL 1970

GIVEN UNDER MY HAND IN THE CITY OF WASHINGTON
THIS SEVENTEENTH DAY OF AUGUST 19 70

John J. Hennessey

JOHN J. HENNESSEY
Major General, USA
Commanding
101st Airborne Division (Airmobile)

Stanley R. Resor

SECRETARY OF THE ARMY

Author was awarded three Bronze Stars with V device

THE UNITED STATES OF AMERICA

TO ALL WHO SHALL SEE THESE PRESENTS, GREETING:

THIS IS TO CERTIFY THAT
THE PRESIDENT OF THE UNITED STATES OF AMERICA
AUTHORIZED BY EXECUTIVE ORDER, FEBRUARY 4, 1944
HAS AWARDED

THE BRONZE STAR MEDAL

TO

SERGEANT JAMES P. BRINKER, ██████, UNITED STATES ARMY

FOR

HEROISM IN GROUND COMBAT

IN THE REPUBLIC OF VIETNAM ON 29 APRIL 1970

GIVEN UNDER MY HAND IN THE CITY OF WASHINGTON
THIS FIFTEENTH DAY OF JULY 19 70

JOHN J. HENNESSEY
Major General, USA
Commanding
101st Airborne Division (Airmobile)

Stanley R. Resor
SECRETARY OF THE ARMY

240

THE UNITED STATES OF AMERICA

TO ALL WHO SHALL SEE THESE PRESENTS, GREETING:

THIS IS TO CERTIFY THAT
THE PRESIDENT OF THE UNITED STATES OF AMERICA
AUTHORIZED BY EXECUTIVE ORDER, FEBRUARY 4, 1944
HAS AWARDED

THE BRONZE STAR MEDAL

(FIRST OAK LEAF CLUSTER)

TO

SERGEANT JAMES P. BRINKER, ███████████, UNITED STATES ARMY

FOR

HEROISM IN GROUND COMBAT

IN THE REPUBLIC OF VIETNAM ON 20 MAY 1970

GIVEN UNDER MY HAND IN THE CITY OF WASHINGTON
THIS   TWELFTH   DAY OF   AUGUST   19 70

JOHN J. HENNESSEY
Major General, USA
Commanding
101st Airborne Division (Airmobile)

SECRETARY OF THE ARMY

241

THE UNITED STATES OF AMERICA

TO ALL WHO SHALL SEE THESE PRESENTS, GREETING:

THIS IS TO CERTIFY THAT
THE PRESIDENT OF THE UNITED STATES OF AMERICA
HAS AWARDED THE

PURPLE HEART

ESTABLISHED BY GENERAL GEORGE WASHINGTON
AT NEWBURGH, NEW YORK, AUGUST 7, 1782

TO

SERGEANT JAMES P. BRINKER, ███████, UNITED STATES ARMY

FOR WOUNDS RECEIVED
IN ACTION

IN THE REPUBLIC OF VIETNAM ON 26 APRIL 1970
GIVEN UNDER MY HAND IN THE CITY OF WASHINGTON
THIS   NINETEENTH   DAY OF   JUNE   19 70

JOHN J. HENNESSEY
Major General, USA
Commanding
101st Airborne Division (Airmobile)

SECRETARY OF THE ARMY

242

THE SOUTH VIETNAM NATIONAL FRONT FOR LIBERATION GIVES LENIENT AND HUMANE TREATMENT TO RALL'ED ARMYMEN AND PRISONERS-OF-WAR

« To welcome puppet officers and soldiers and puppet officials back to the just cause ; show leniency and give humane treatment to rallied armymen and prisoners-of-war.

☆ Captured officers and soldiers of the puppet army will enjoy humane treatment and leniency,

☆ Men in the US army and its satellite armies who cross over to the peoples side will be given kind treatment and helped to return to their families when conditions permit.

☆ Captured U.S. and satellite troops will receive the same treatment as captured puppet troops..., »

(Article 12 of the SVNNFL'S Political programme)

HOW TO SURRENDER OR TO CROSS OVER TO THE NFL's SIDE

— Gun on the ground or slung across the back

— Hands up above the head

— If still at some distance from the Liberation troops, tie a white cloth to the tip of your gun.

CÁCH ĐẦU HÀNG HOẶC KHI CHẠY SANG PHÍA MẶT TRẬN D.T.G.P.

— Bỏ súng xuống đất hoặc khoác chéo sau lưng.

— Dơ tay cao quá đầu.

— Nếu còn cách xa quân Giải phóng, buộc một mảnh vải trắng vào đầu súng.

Truyền đơn giải thích chính sách tù hàng binh dành cho binh sĩ Mỹ.

NVA surrender pamphlet

243

Chiêu Hoi pamphlets

Dog Tag

Propaganda Stamp
from dead NVA, Hill 882

Brave Eagle coin

Korean laundry shop patch

CIB — Combat Infantryman's subdued Badge

5th Division

502nd Infantry Crest

ID Card

Funny MPC Money

Viet Nam Driver's License

Glossary

45: A Colt 45 caliber pistol, M1911A1

51: A Communist bloc 51 caliber 12.7mm anti-aircraft machine gun

Airmobile: A unit that can be moved frequently by helicopter

AIT: Advanced Infantry Training; the training an infantry soldier receives after Basic Training.

AK-47: A Communist bloc 30 round full automatic assault rifle

AK-50: A sappers modified AK with a folding stock

AO: Area of Operations; the assigned territory of a unit

APC: Armored Personnel Carrier; a lightly armored vehicle for carrying about ten soldiers

APO: Army Post Office; a blind delivery address used to send mail to soldiers

Arkie: Someone from Arkansas

ARVN: Army Viet Nam; a soldier of South Viet Nam or Republic of Viet Nam.

B52: A high altitude bomber; dump truck; a beer opener

Basic Training: The first training that virtually all soldiers receive no matter what their MOS is

Bastogne: A town in Belgium; the scene of a great battle by 101st Airborne Division

BDE: A group of three or four BNs in Vietnam era

Beaucoup: French for many or much; Vietnamese assume all Americans speak French

BN: Battalion; A group of six companies in Viet Nam era

Body Bag: A plastic zippered large green bag used to place remains of fallen soldier

Boonie Cap: A loose and ragged hat that shades sun and adds to camouflage

Boonie Rat: Grunt; GI; an infantryman living in the jungle

Boot Camp: Basic Training

Brass: Officer, usually a Major or higher

Buck Sergeant: A Sergeant E-5; lowest ranking Sergeant; usually a squad leader

Bush: "The bush;" boonies, jungle

Buy the Farm; Buy the Ranch: To die in combat

C4: A plastic explosive

Camp Eagle: A perimeter camp southwest of Hue that contained the 1st Brigade and other units of the 101st Airborne Division. In reference to "Old Abe," the Screaming Eagle on the Division patch

Charlie Rats: C-Rations

Cherry: A new guy or a virgin to combat

Chink: Derogatory term for a Chinese person

Chopper: All helicopters

Chu Hoi: A program offering amnesty to enemy soldiers who desert

CO: Commanding Officer; Old Man

Concertina: An Italian word for a circular wire with razor-sharp attachments

Cooking off: 1. An overheated weapon firing without the trigger being pulled 2. Holding a grenade a few seconds after releasing the pin handle before throwing it into a bunker

Claymore: An anti-personnel mine named after a Scottish sword

Click: 1 kilometer

Click Corners: The intersecting corners of square kilometers on a military map

Cobra: A modified, heavily armed Huey with a smaller body

CP: Command Post; a units top officer, Sergeant and radiomen.

CSM: Command Sergeant Major, High-ranking NCO

Daisy Chain: A string of claymore mines connected by a Detonation Cord

Dee Dee or Dee Dee Mau: Vietnamese for getting away quick

Dee Dee trail: A side trail where an NVA soldier can make his escape

Delta: The far southern part of Viet Nam where the Mekong River flows into South China Sea

DMZ: Demilitarized Zone; the area between North and South Viet Nam. A misnomer in political and military terms

Death Card: A calling card left on the body of an enemy soldier

Det Cord: Detonation Cord; a cord made of C4 that could connect multiple mines or charges together

Deuce and a half: A two and one half-ton truck frequently used to transport troops

Dew: Cannabis, Marijuana.

Dink: Vulgar term for enemy soldier; Gook; from short stature

Dinky or Dinky Dow: Vietnamese for you are crazy or loony

Donut Dolly: A condescending term for a Red Cross girl

Drag: Last man in a column of soldiers; tail

Draftee: A conscript; someone forced into military service.

Dust off: A Huey helicopter used to carry wounded soldiers; also Medivac

Dutch Courage: Courage under the influence of alcohol

Fatigue: A soldier's field shirt; Jungle fatigue, Camouflage fatigue

FNG: F**king new guy; Cherry

FO: Forward Observer; an officer or trained enlisted man that calls in and adjusts artillery or mortars

Frag: Fragmentation grenade; M-26, M-33

Freedom Bird: The chartered aircraft that will take a soldier home

Friendlies: Your own or allied troops

FSB: Fire Support Base; a perimeter containing artillery, mortars, CP and defenses

Gook: Vulgar term for a Viet Cong or North Vietnamese soldier. A derogatory term for an Asian; possibly from megook, a poor pronunciation of American used by Koreans.

Grunt: A GI; an infantryman

Hamburger Hill: Dong Ap Bia; a mountain on west side of A Shau valley; battle fought in May 1969 with over 100% casualties

HE: High Explosive; a standard artillery round

Head: Short for pothead or person who smokes marijuana

Heliport: An LZ in the rear

HHC: Headquarters and Headquarters Company; Company of a BN. Early in Vietnam War contained Weapons Platoon and Recondo Platoon

Ho Chi Minh: Leader of North Viet Nam; also Ho, Uncle Ho

Honcho: Head man or boss; term from Korea

Horn: Radio

Huey: A UH-1D utility helicopter; Slick

249

Indo-China: A French term for the area of Viet Nam, Cambodia, and Laos

Juicer: Person who drinks alcohol instead of smoking marijuana

Jump School: A school to train paratroopers

KIA: Killed in Action; sometimes KIHA: Killed in Hostile Action

Kill Zone: An area during combat with little or no cover; the area where weapons are most effective

Kit Carson Scout: A former VC or NVA that works as a scout for American troops

Lance Corporal: Marine Corps equivalent of an Army PFC

LAW: Disposable Light Anti-Tank Weapon; akin to an RPG

LZ: Landing Zone; a place where helicopters can land

LBJ: Long Binh Jail; A dangerous military prison in Viet Nam

LOH: Light Observation Helicopter, loach; a small helicopter used for both Reconnaissance and as a small gunship

LP: Listening Post; a dangerous position outside of a units night defensive perimeter manned by two guys to listen and watch for enemy activity

LRRP: Long Range Reconnaissance Patrol

L.T.: A Lieutenant; usually a Platoon Leader

M-14: A medium single, semi-automatic, or automatic rifle used early in Vietnam but replaced by the M16 rifle. 7.62mm

M16: A light assault rifle, single semi-automatic, automatic, used during the Vietnam War. 5.56mm

M60: A crew-served medium machine gun

M-79: A 40mm grenade launcher or canister shotgun

Mai Lai: A village south of Da Nang where over 200 men, women, and children were slaughtered by poorly led American troops

MIA: Missing in Action

Million Dollar Wound: A serious, but non-life threatening wound that will keep a soldier from returning to war

MOS: Main Occupational Specialty; a description of your job in the military

MP: Military Police; shore Patrol in Navy

MPC: Military Payment Certificates; "Funny Money"; money substitute used in war zone

MRE: Meal Ready to Eat; present-day replacement for C-Rations

Nam: Short for Viet Nam; sometimes called "The Nam"

NCO: Non-Commissioned Officer; a Corporal or Sergeant

NCOCS: Non Commissioned Officer Candidate School; a school similar to OCS that's purpose is to train Sergeants; sometimes called shake and bakes

NDP: Night Defensive Position; the place where a unit stays the night

NDT: Night Defensive Target; pre adjusted artillery targets near a unit's NDP

Number one: What a Vietnamese calls you if he likes you

Number ten: What a Vietnamese calls you if he doesn't like you

Nuoc Mam: A fermented fish powder and sauce

NVA: North Vietnamese Army.

OCS: Officer Candidate School; training to become an officer. Usually for those with a college degree or some college

Old Abe: The name of the eagle on the patch of the 101st Airborne Division; named after a mascot of a Civil War Wisconsin Regiment

Old Man: Commanding Officer

On Line Assault: A military maneuver where a line of standing soldiers move forward using heavy fire to move up on enemy defensive positions

OP: Observation Position; a position out a short distance from a unit when stopped during the daytime

P38: A small can opener that is in C-Ration cases

Pacification: A program of the RVN government to move villagers into defensible villages in order to stop them from supplying men and food to the enemy

Pack Number: A number assigned to a soldier to identify him over the radio without using his name

PFC: Private First Class; E-3 An experienced or fully trained Private; not usually a leadership position

PL: Platoon Leader; usually a 1st Lieutenant

PLT: Platooon; a unit of three squads and a CP. About thirty men

Point Man: The lead man in a moving column of soldiers

Poncho Liner: A polyester blanket that can be strapped to the inside of a rain poncho

POW: Prisoner of War

Psych-Ops: Psychological operations; using non-combat methods to demoralize or misinform the enemy

PTSD: Post-Traumatic Stress Disorder; psychological problems long after actual incident

PX: Post Exchange; Military General Store

RA: Regular Army; a full-time professional soldier who was not drafted or part time like NG or AR

R&R: Rest and Recuperation; a one-week leave given to soldiers usually after six months of overseas duty

REMF: Rear Echelon Mother F**ker

Ricans: US soldiers from Puerto Rico

ROTC: Reserve Officer Training Corp; training to become an officer while in college

Round eye: A non-Asian girl or woman

RPD: A small machine gun used by the Communist bloc

RPG-2: A small anti-tank rocket and shape charge frequently used in Vietnam as an anti-personnel weapon by Communist forces

RTO: Radio Telephone Operator

RVN: Republic of Viet Nam; the former country, also known as South Viet Nam

S2 S3: Operations and Intelligence at Battalion level

Sancho Panza: A short stocky Hispanic

Sapper: In the American Army, an Engineer; NVA or VC that infiltrated perimeters

Satchel Charge: A small block of explosives used by VC and NVA; equivalent of an American concussion grenade

SEAL: A Navy Commando

See the elephant: A term used by one who has overcome great difficulties or obstacles

SERTs: Screaming Eagle Replacement and Training. In Vietnam, training before being sent to your unit in the 101st Airborne Division

Sh*thook: Chinook or CH-47 dual rotor cargo helicopter

SKS: A semi-automatic rifle used by the Communist forces

Smoke grenade: A grenade that gives over one of several colored smoke; used to mark a units position or verify a unit
Starlight Scope: An observation or riflescope that amplifies very dim light into a green and black visible image
Strike Force: A name for the 2/502 infantry from WWII until the present
Tail Gunner: Machine gunner in the tail or rear of a B-17 or B-24 Bomber in WWII
Tet: A Vietnamese Buddhist Holiday
Texican: A Texan of Mexican ancestry
TOC: Tactical Operations Center; the planning room of a larger unit
TOP: A Sergeant First Class; usually the highest-ranking Sergeant in a line company
Trident: A three-forked spear used on the insignia of a Navy SEAL
Trip Flare: A booby trap-like magnesium flare that is used to alert a unit that the enemy is near
VC: Viet Cong; Communist forces from South Viet Nam
Veghel: A town in Netherlands; scene of WWII battle by 101st Airborne
Widowmaker: A booby trap or mechanical ambush using a claymore mine
Widowmakers: A name for those of the 502nd Airborne Division
Willie Peter: White phosphorus grenade or artillery projectile
World: The United States of America; home. Implying that Vietnam isn't really part of the world
XM: Experimental Model; a new weapon under evaluation
XO: Executive officer or second in command
Yellow Brick Road: The main north-south road in A Shau valley; any large trail in the jungle.